How To Run A Baske___ ___amp:
A Guide to Directing a Successful Basketball Camp

Dan Spainhour

Educational Coaching & Business Communications, Naples, Florida

www.ecbcommunications.com

How To Run A Basketball Camp:
A Guide to Directing a Successful Basketball Camp

By: Dan Spainhour

ISBN 978-0-6151-4329-3

Educational Coaching & Business Communications

7921 Umberto Court
Naples, FL 34414

About the Author

Dan Spainhour has more than 20 years of high school and college coaching experience. Coach Spainhour has been directing camps for over 18 years.

Coach Spainhour has received numerous awards during his coaching career, including three state championships and fourteen coach of the year honors. As a high school basketball coach he has collected over 230 victories and has won nearly 70% of his games. Spainhour most recently worked at Florida State as the Director of Basketball Operations. He was involved in all phases of the day-to-day operations of the men's basketball office. He handled the office and team fiscal matters, team travel, academic development, dining and housing contracts and served as the director of the annual Leonard Hamilton basketball camp for boys. He also coached at the University of Miami where he worked under current Florida State coach, Leonard Hamilton. During his time at Miami he helped lead the Hurricanes to their first NCAA tournament appearance in 38 years. Coach Spainhour is considered one of the top teachers of basketball fundamentals in the country. He instructed for Coach Mike Krzyzewski's camps for ten years. He has also worked camps across the country for legendary coaches such as Morgan Wootten and John Thompson.

He is the founder of Educational Coaching and Business Communications, a company that specializes in informational manuals for educators, parents, coaches and athletes. He is the author of three books--*How to Get Your Child An Athletic Scholarship: A Parent's Guide to Recruiting; A Season in Words: A Coach's Guide to Motivation from the Preseason to the Postseason;* and *How to Run A Basketball Camp: A Guide to a Successful Basketball Camp.* Spainhour is also the founder and director of the East Coast Basketball Camp, which is now one of the most renowned basketball camps in the Mid-Atlantic.

Spainhour was the recipient of the Governor's Laurel Wreath Award as an Ambassador of Athletics in the State of North Carolina. He was appointed to the state's agency governing private school athletics and elected to the committee which oversaw state sectional basketball tournaments in the state during his career. He earned his bachelor's degree in health and physical education from High Point College and his Master's Degree in sports administration from the University of Miami . He is married to the former Cara Giese and resides in Naples, Florida.

Table of Contents

Introduction

Background

My first experience with a basketball camp came as a young child. I remember my family loading up the station wagon and heading two hours to Campbell College's annual basketball camp located in Buies Creek, NC. At the time Campbell's camp was considered to be one of the best in the state. Each year the staff would be filled with outstanding college coaches and players. I remember Lefty Driesell giving a speech and his point guard, John Lucas being at the camp. It was a great experience—one that remains vivid to this day.

I began directing camps nearly 20 years ago when I started coaching high school basketball at Bishop McGuinness High School. I founded East Coast Basketball Camps in 1998 after I returned to high school coaching from the University of Miami. The camp has developed into one of the top day camps in North Carolina. Each summer we instruct hundreds of students.

Over the years, I have had many coaching friends contact me to discuss starting a camp of their own. I have met with many of them and we've talked about starting and running a basketball camp. After awhile I began to wonder how many other coaches could benefit from having a "how-to" manual for conducting a basketball camp. Thus the idea for this instructional manual was born.

The purpose of this manual is to provide you with a guide for conducting your own camp. If you are currently holding a camp this guide can give you some ideas that may improve your camp. If you are considering starting a camp then this guide will take you step-by-step through the development of a camp.

It is designed to show you how we started and how we conduct East Coast Basketball Camps. You will find everything you need to run a successful camp year after year.

Determine Your Objectives

What do you want to accomplish with your camp? That's the best place to start when developing a camp. Hopefully, the number one goal is to teach young people the fundamentals necessary to play basketball and instill good habits both on and off the court. Many coaches may have other objectives as well. East Coast Basketball Camps' (ECBC) first and foremost objective is to instill an enthusiasm about basketball to our campers while providing them with methods and skills required to become better basketball players. The first thing you should do before starting a camp is write out your goals.

Many high school coaches use camps as a developmental tool for their own program. A coach can begin to teach fundamentals of his program to youngsters at an early age if he can get future players in his camp. If this is your primary objective, then you may want to target only students that will be in your program.

Unfortunately, some coaches run camps strictly to make money. I'm not going to be misleading. If East Coast Basketball Camps did not make a profit, we wouldn't be running many camps. But if your main goal is to turn a huge profit, you'll find yourself cutting corners and that in turn will shortchange the campers. Keep your primary objective targeted toward the campers and your camp will always be a hit. Target your objective toward yourself and the campers will pick up on it.

Why Run a Camp?

There are many reasons to consider running a camp. If you are a coach, running a camp is an excellent way to get your players in the gym in the summer. Using your players as counselors is also a great way for them to develop a sense of ownership of your program. Younger children look up to the older counselors, which gives your players a sense of pride about being in your program.

Using your players as counselors is beneficial because your players gain a greater understanding of the game through teaching. It's been said, you learn more through teaching than by doing. I have seen many of my players' "aha lights" click on from a direct result of teaching the game to younger children.

Camps also allow your program to develop a presence in the community. Going to your basketball camp can be a big deal for young children. It makes them more excited about some day being a member of your program.

Another reason to consider running a camp is if you simply enjoy teaching the game. One of the things I've learned through my years of coaching is that true coaches love teaching the game. I never really got caught up in the other aspects involved with coaching. But the chance to teach the game has always excited me and that is what our basketball camps do—they allow me to continue to teach the game.

And of course, there are financial reasons to run a camp. Most coaches are grossly underpaid. Camps can provide a nice addition to your coaching supplement. Camps can be very profitable. That's why there are so many held each year. Just make sure that you are not cheating the campers by becoming greedy or that you start to cut corners to save a few bucks.

Qualities Needed

- Enthusiasm—There's an old saying that states enthusiasm is caught not taught. The most important characteristic to have —even more so than basketball knowledge—is enthusiasm. You will have a successful camp if you can generate a sense of excitement about your camp.

- Knowledge—Directing a basketball camp without an understanding of basic basketball fundamentals is akin to teaching a French course when you only speak English. This guide will provide you with assistance to make your teaching easier but you still need the basic basketball background before your camp will be a tremendous success.

- Teaching ability—Having stated the need for knowledge the next most important attribute is the ability to impart your knowledge to your campers. Effective communication is essential in any type of student-teacher situation. There isn't one definitive measure to ensure effective communication. The important thing is to communicate in a manner that is consistent with your personality. The lectures and other formats found here will be of assistance but it will be up to you to find what personality trait best suits you to ensure that your campers are receptive to what they're being taught at your camp.

- Willingness to interact— Because of the responsibilities placed upon the camp director, it is easy to allow your counselors to provide most of the interaction with the campers. I've seen camps—even ones named after the director themselves—where the camp director may give a lecture or two but other than that they have very little interaction with the campers. Since it is your camp, campers and parents expect you to be very involved in teaching and monitoring the campers. Therefore, as camp director you must be eager to interact with all campers and parents.

About This Guide

You'll find in this guide everything you need for your very own basketball camp. It will save you time since forms, schedules, lectures etc. are provided and can easily be copied. East Coast Basketball Camps are week long camps that run from 8:30 am to 3:00 pm each day. The schedules found here are based upon our format. The focus of this guide is to provide you with ideas and formats for conducting a productive camp. Obviously, schedules and other items can be adjusted to fit your needs.

Section
One

Laying the Groundwork

Naming Your Camp & Other Business Details

What you decide to name your camp will probably be based upon your objective of holding a camp. If your main purpose is to promote your own program, then you may want to call it your school's name. As a high school coach, I always tried to avoid using the school's name simply because of the financial concerns that may occur. I know of coaches who have conducted camps under the name of their school and later school personnel or the school board wanted to know where the money was. The school claimed that since it was a school camp they were entitled to the money and the coach should be paid a supplement for running the camp. If you plan to use the school's name meet will all parties beforehand to establish financial expectations. An alternative is to invent a name for your camp and then plan to rent your facility. If you can't think of a name, you could always name it after yourself.. Establish your camp as a business once you decide upon the name by opening a separate checking account. Many people are cautious of sending a check to a person. It is also much easier to keep your records straight if you have a separate account.

> ☞
> *Take time to think about what you want to accomplish with your camp and then work to make your camp meet that objective.*

I have always preferred to name a camp something other than the school name. One reason is when you are going through the school then you may have to go through their financial office to pay your coaches and deposit your checks. I have found it is much easier to keep everything separate from the school.

Locating a Site

One of the first steps for your camp is finding a site to hold it. Some school systems may allow you to use the gym free of charge. As stated in the previous paragraph make sure all particulars are agreed upon beforehand.

Other school systems may charge a reduced rate for its personnel. When talking with school officials let them know that you will carry your own insurance and that your insurance company will provide them with a certificate of liability insurance listing them as an additional insured party— more on insurance later. Sometimes providing the school with your own insurance can lower the rental fee.

Most facilities' fees will be based either on a flat rental fee or a percentage total for each camper. There are advantages and disadvantages to both methods. When you pay a flat fee you will need to get enough campers to cover the rental costs. Most school systems operate on a flat fee based upon your number of hours of usage. Fees normally range from $20/hr to $60/hr. I have had some schools quote me a price as high as $250/hr. Paying a rental fee is okay if you are fairly certain of the number of campers you will get. I don't mind paying a reasonable rental fee at places where our camps are established.

The other method we use for site rental is paying on a percentage basis. I always try to negotiate a percentage at places where we are just starting out for two reasons. First, and foremost, I don't want to lock myself into a high rental fee when I don't know how many campers I will have. Secondly, if the site is receiving a percentage based on the number of campers enrolled then their incentive to recruit campers is greater. I prefer to use a percentage with all YMCA's & YWCA's that we use. This way the Y's are more apt to promote the camp among their members since more campers equal more money.

I negotiate a percent using a couple of methods. I prefer to offer a lower percentage (around 15% per camper) and I handle everything. Everything means mailings, hiring coaches, buying t-shirts, etc. In these deals, East Coast Basketball Camps will provide the site with brochures and flyers and they make them available. If the negotiated percentage is large (30-50 percent) then I allow the site to handle everything. I will still hire the coaches but the site will pay them. They will also buy the T-shirts and are responsible for getting the word out to the campers. This method works particularly well when you are considering holding a camp out of town.

You may ask why don't you always work on a percentage basis? Answer—economics. Let's say you negotiate a percentage deal of 20 percent per camper and your tuition rate is $100. If you have 150 campers then your rent would be $3000 ($20 x 150). You can rent some very nice places for $3000 a week.

On the other hand, let's say you only have 20 campers. The percentage format would cost you only $400 in rent. The key to finding a site is doing your homework. Be careful not to take the first offer. What sounds like a small amount can quickly grow into a huge sum of money.

Things to Negotiate

As they say "everything is negotiable". When trying to secure a site, it is best to keep that thought in mind. Following are some things to negotiate that may result in a lower rental fee.

- Concession sales. Many sites have their own drink and snack machines from which they receive a substantial profit. I have used this in our negotiations many times. I tell the facility that our camps normally run their own concessions and that we have a full time staff member hired just for this responsibility. I then tell them that I am willing to shut down concessions and allow campers to use the facilities' vending machines for a lower rental fee.

- Discounted tuition rate for the facilities' students or members. This is particularly effective when dealing with YMCA's or other facilities that have their own membership. Normally the tuition is discounted 15-20% depending upon how much the facility agrees to reduce the rent.

Once both parties agree to the rental terms it is advisable to sign a contract. Even if you agree that you will not be charged a rental fee, it is best to sign a contract. I once ran a week of camp at a small private school where the principal and I were friends. Since the campers were primarily students from the school the principal agreed to allow us to use their gym free of charge. Two months after the camp the athletic boosters president contacted me wanting to know why I hadn't paid for using their gym. The boosters went to the principal demanding a huge rental fee—more than any facility we had ever used. They were very threatening and forced the principal to ask for payment. Obviously, I protested but I eventually sent a donation for use of the gym. If I had a contract stating our terms, this would have been prevented.

- *Consider using a percentage format for camps just starting out or if your enrollment is small.*

- *Use a flat rental fee when your camp is established or you are sure of a large enrollment.*

- *Sign a contract— even when working among friends.*

Location, Location, Location

Just as it is with real estate, the location of your camp will have a huge effect on your camps' success. Consider locations where you have name recognition first. If parents know you, they'll be more likely to send their child to your camp.

Also check the number of camps in the area. An area that has several basketball camps running in a week may hurt your enrollment possibilities. Some of the best locations may be small rural towns where there are very few camps. Often in larger towns you will have more competition.

Dates

Always check the local schools' calendars to ensure that students are not in school during the week(s) that you want to have your camp. Be careful about planning a camp too close to the end of the school year. In areas where the school year may be extended due to inclement weather you may find yourself without campers. You also may want to avoid the week of July 4th. Other than that, with proper planning and marketing any week can be an effective week.

Ages/Sex

What ages and sex do you want your campers to be? I have tried many combinations of ages ranging from 6-18. Our camps are now open to any boy or girl ages 8-18. While most of our campers are between ages 10-16, I don't mind having younger or older campers. I have found that if you go below age 8 you tend to have problems keeping their attention for the entire day. Once again, it is important to determine your primary objective of your camp. If you are just trying to get kids involved and are willing to provide a day care type camp then opening it up to younger children is fine. I just feel that younger than 8 makes it more difficult to really teach basketball, which is what I want our camps to be about. You may want to consider half day camps if you accept campers younger than 8.

On the other end of the spectrum, we once had a rising ninth grade age limit. I did this because many of the counselors were my high school players and we wanted an age separation between our coaches and counselors. Now, I allow all high school students and we still have some high school players serve as counselors. I simply put the high school counselors with the younger players and the older coaches with the high school kids.

Your camp objectives should also determine whether your camp will be coed. Our camps are coed. When deciding upon the objective of our camps, I wanted to provide every camper within a fun-filled atmosphere all the skills necessary to become a better basketball player. I thought why should that apply only to boys so from the very beginning we made East Coast Basketball Camps a coed camp and we have never regretted the decision. Depending upon enrollment and available space, we normally put the younger boys and girls together and have a separate girls and boys division for the older campers . But even when our numbers don't allow any separation we have never had any problems. It works very well for us but you will have to decide what's best for you.

Tuition

Reaching a decision on what to charge can be a trying experience. While you don't want to over charge you also don't want to lose money either. There are many costs involved in running a camp. Prizes, t-shirts, staff wages, facility fees and insurance are some of the largest expenses.

Do some research and try to determine what other people are charging for camps in your area before deciding upon the costs of your camp . Currently, East Coast Basketball Camps' tuition rates range from $125 to $180 per week depending upon the location. We offer a $10 discount for campers from the same family and to any camper who attends multiple weeks.

Parents will not mind paying the going rate to send their child to your camp if your camp is of high quality .

Deposits

Determining whether you will require a deposit, full tuition or nothing when campers pre-register is a matter of personal choice. East Coast Basketball Camps' policy is to require full payment when the child sends in his/her registration materials. We include the following statement on our brochures:

To ensure that each child receives the individual attention necessary for improvement we often must stop accepting applications once we reach our capacity. To reserve your spot, please include complete payment with your application. Space is reserved on a first come basis.

Because all of your planning and hiring of counselors depends upon the number of enrolled campers, the earlier you know the number of campers the better. By paying full tuition, there is less of a chance that a camper will not attend.

Refunds

Once again it is a matter of choice. ECBC's policy is the following:

A refund less $50 for administrative costs can be requested until the camp starting date. After this date, no refunds will be given. All refunds must be requested in a written statement via email or regular mail.

When you first start your camp, you may think you'll satisfy every refund request. Consider the following example. A camp was planned to be held at a middle school. The school required a flat rental fee which had to be paid in advance. The camp had a great pre-registration period but the majority of the campers were students at the school. Two weeks before the camp the director learned that a week-long local "summer-fest" for students originally scheduled for an earlier week was moved because of inclement weather to the same week as his camp. Cancellations began to come in because the students wanted to be involved in the festival. Since he did not have a refund policy, he was forced to give the full refund. Needless to say, the camp lost money.

Insurance

In today's litigious society, doing anything without being properly insured is setting yourself up for potential disaster. Nothing can put you out of business quicker than a lawsuit. No matter how careful you are things can still happen.

An insurance program protects you and your staff against bodily injury and property damage claims due to alleged negligence. The program also protects your campers with accident medical insurance. You can expect to pay between $2.50-$6.00 per camper which is certainly worth the investment.

Here are three companies that specializes in camp insurance:

- Francis L. Dean
  1776 S. Naperville Road
  PO Box 4200
  Wheaton, IL 60189
  (800) 745-2409
  www.fdean.com

- Summit America
  7400 College Blvd.
  Overland Park, KS 66210
  (800) 955-1991
  www.summitamerica-ins.com

- The Camp Team
  7615 W 38th Ave. Suite B109
  Wheat Ridge, CO 80033
  (800) 747-9573
  www.campteam.com

Ask the company to provide a certificate of insurance and list the camp facility as additionally insured.

Personnel

The quality of your camp will hinge on the quality of your staff. I always tell our counselors at the pre-camp meeting that the success of the week will be depend on them. Campers hopefully will remember some of the things you teach but they undoubtedly will remember their interaction with the coaches.

For that reason alone, I always try to hire some younger counselors. College students are my first choice but I also don't mind using current high school players for help with the younger campers. Using your players is a good idea if you are a high school or college coach.

Also try to recruit local coaches—high school, middle school, recreation. Assistant coaches often make very good camp counselors because they are excited to learn and eager to show their knowledge. My philosophy is to hire enthusiastic coaches regardless of their experience. As you will see later, our camp format is such that I ensure the proper fundamentals and techniques are being taught. I provide each coach

Things to look for when hiring your staff

- *Teaching ability*

- *Enthusiasm*

- *Knowledge*

- *Coaching experience*

- *Playing experience*

with a step-by-step teaching method to make sure everything is being taught correctly. Therefore, I would much rather hire a young enthusiastic coach with limited knowledge as opposed to one who may be more experienced but not as enthusiastic.

Try to keep your player-to-coach ratio at 10:1. Depending upon the size of your camp, it may be a good idea to hire an experienced coach as your assistant to help oversee the running of the camp. A good assistant can help alleviate a lot of problems that may arise. This will also help you have time to interact with campers and parents.

In the *Camp Materials, Section Five* portion of this book there is a personnel sheet you can use to guarantee that you have adequate coverage for your camp week. Counselors can be assigned to more than one responsibility but should be assigned to one team and one teaching station.

T-shirts/Giveaways

An important aspect of every basketball camp is the t-shirt the campers receive. Not only are the shirts something the campers enjoy having but they also provide an excellent marketing opportunity for your camp. T-shirts provide for name recognition and the more your camp is recognized the more interest is generated.

Consider seeking a sponsor for your t-shirts. A local business may be willing to pay for the shirts in exchange for placing their name on the back of your shirt.

> *Avoid putting the date on your camp t-shirt. This way you can use leftover t-shirts for future camps.*

Another thing to decide is what you will use as giveaways and prizes for your campers. We give certificates (see *Camp Materials Section 5*) to our skills contest winners and for other individual accomplishments. We also give a hustler of the day , Mr. & Mrs. Enthusiasm, & an Attitude certificate each day. We do not give awards for league or tournament champions. This is a matter of personal taste. While the games are important, we want the focus of our camp to be on learning and instruction. We try to treat our games as an opportunity to implement the morning instruction into team play. We have found that the more emphasis that is placed on the outcome of the games the less likely the campers are to try new things. Again, this is simply our way of doing it and it has worked for us.

Certificates

If you choose to give certificates to your contests winners you can easily print them on your computer. Otherwise you may want to have some printed or purchase generic ones.

A copy of the certificates we use in found in the *Section Five—Camp Materials*. We design it and print it on certificate paper using Microsoft Publisher before camp. We handwrite the recognized campers' names and give them out at the end of camp each day.

Equipment needed

Size matters when it comes to equipment. The larger your enrollment the more equipment you will need. Below is a basic checklist of the equipment you'll need for your camp.

Equipment Checklist

_____ Basketballs—You will need more during the stations portion of camp and fewer during the games. A good ratio is about 1 basketball for every 5 campers.

_____Baskets—At least one full court. Six baskets is preferred.

_____Cones—used for drills & contests. Minimum of six.

_____Pennies (practice jerseys)—Its best to avoid playing shirts and skins at all times. Many young boys are very self-conscious and do not want to take their shirts off. At least 10 pennies are needed.

_____Jump ropes—Primarily for demonstration purposes. 2 needed.

_____Television, VCR or DVD player—One needed.

_____Video-camera (optional).

_____Instructional Videotapes/DVD's

_____Highlight videotapes/DVD's

_____Whistles

_____Stopwatches

Section Two

Marketing

You can have the best basketball camp in town but if no one knows about it you'll never be successful. If you're like most coaches you don't have a lot of money to spend on advertising. This section is not meant to be a marketing course but you'll be much more successful if you commit to some advertising.

The best type of advertising is FREE advertising. Other than the cost of printing our brochures and flyers and some mailings, East Coast Basketball Camps does not pay for any advertising. If you have a large budget then you may want to buy ad space in the newspaper or on radio or TV. A lot of camps do and it seems to work for them. But my philosophy is simple—the more we pay out the less we have.

Here are the advertising methods that I have found to be most effective:

Brochures

We print our own brochures from the computer. It is designed on the Publisher Program. Once we have our brochures completed we put them everywhere we can think of. Here are some places you should consider placing your camp brochures:

- Mail to campers from previous years
- Mail to local youth leagues. Try to get names and addresses from youth league officials.
- Facility where the camp will occur.
- On car windshields at little league fields and other youth sports events.
- Car windshields at AAU tournaments.
- Local business counters.
- Elementary schools.
- Middle schools.
- High schools.

On the following page is a sample brochure. It is a tri-fold brochure that is mail-ready. This eliminates the need for envelopes which helps reduce mailing costs.

Register online at www.eastcoastbasketballcamps.com or mail
check for $150 to
East Coast Basketball Camp
PO Box 57
King, NC 27021
(Please Print)

Name _____

Address _____

City, State, Zip _____

E-mail _____
(you will receive an email confirmation of your enrollment)

T-shirt size _____

Phone _____ Emergency no. _____

Age as of 1st day of camp _____ Height _____

Grade in 2006-2007 School Year _____

M/F _____ School attending now _____

I waive and release East Coast Basketball Camps from any and all liability from injury and illness going to camp from home or while at camp or while returning home. I, as parent/guardian, have actual knowledge and appreciation of the particulars of the program and hereby voluntarily consent to said minor's participation, and assume the risk arising therefrom. I hereby give my permission for emergency medical treatment in the event I cannot be reached.

East Coast Camps requires a physical examination within the 12 month period of the date the camper is scheduled to attend camp. I confirm that my child will meet this requirement and I will notify East Coast Basketball Camps of any condition that may prevent him/her from participating in any/all camp activities.

Signature of Parent/Guardian: _____

Date: _____

Family Discount $10.00
(Receive a **$10** discount for each additional immediate (brother/ sister) family member enrolled)
Refund Policy: A refund less **$50** for administrative costs can be requested until the camp starting date. After this date, no refunds will be given. All refunds must be requested in a written statement.

East Coast Basketball Camps
PO Box 57
King, NC 27021

2006
East Coast Basketball
Camp
For Boys and Girls
Ages 8-18

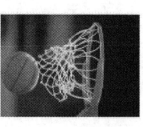

at West Stokes High School
King, NC
July 10-14

Directed by Dan Spainhour

*5 Full Days of Great
Basketball Instruction*
$150
www.eastcoastbasketballcamps.com
(850) 264-3333

Typical Daily Schedule
Each Day is Packed With Basketball!

8:30-8:50 Morning Instructions & Stretching
8:50-9:10 Fundamental Instructions/Demonstrations
9:10-10:35 Stations—Individual Fundamental Work
10:35-10:55 Skills Contests
10:55-11:10 Fundamental Practice Session—Campers are shown how to practice for maximum improvement
11:10-11:30 3 on 3 league play
11:30-12:00 Lunch
12:00-12:30 Set the Camp Record Contests
12:30-12:50 Guest Speaker/Video Session
12:50-1:20 Shooting Clinic
1:20-1:40 Evaluation Drills
1:40-2:00 Hot Shot Competition
2:00-2:50 League Games
2:50-3:00 Review & Closing Lecture

Camp Features

- Quality fundamental instruction
- Each camper receives a Camp T-Shirt
- Daily skills contests and prizes
- Set the camp record contests in which campers have an opportunity to enter into East Coast Basketball's Hall of Champions

Goal of the Camp

"The goal of our camp is to provide every camper, within a fun-filled atmosphere, the basic fundamentals necessary to play basketball. We emphasize the fundamentals. Every camper will be shown what to practice and more importantly HOW TO PRACTICE. Everyone will receive plenty of individual attention. We want each camper to be a better player when the week is over."

Coach Dan Spainhour

Register online at
www.eastcoastbasketballcamps.com

Before you can excel at the high school or college level you must first master the fundamentals. We teach the fundamentals and provide each camper with individual instruction in all phases of the game!

THE CAMP

During the morning session, time will be devoted to the development of individual skills. Campers will be schooled in all aspects of individual offensive and defensive basketball during teaching stations. These stations will cover shooting, ball handling, passing, screening, and man-to-man defense. Each camper will receive loads of "hands-on" experience as they go through various drills aimed at teaching the proper techniques of the game of basketball.

Following stations, campers will be shown how to properly practice during the fundamental practice session. This session demonstrates how to practice individually to improve important fundamentals required to become better basketball players.

Each morning, Coach Spainhour will cover topics such as communication, self-improvement, how to practice and what coaches look for in players.

League games, arranged by age groups, are devoted to developing the team concept and the incorporation of the skills learned during teaching stations. Also, campers will compete in skills contests by age group.

Campers should bring a bag lunch. Drinks will be sold at the camp site.

Dan Spainhour

The camp is directed by Florida State's Dan Spainhour. Coach Spainhour has been directing camps for over 20 years. He has received numerous awards during his coaching career, including three state championships and fourteen coach of the year honors. This season he served as Director of Basketball Operations for the FSU Seminoles where he helped lead them to the postseason NIT. As a high school basketball coach, he collected over 230 victories and won nearly 70% of his games. He also coached at the University of Miami where he helped lead the Hurricanes to their first NCAA tournament appearance in 38 years.

Coach Spainhour is considered to be one of the top teachers of basketball fundamentals in the country. He instructed for Coach Mike Krzyzewski's camps for ten years. He has worked camps across the country for legendary coaches such as Morgan Wootten and John Thompson. He is the founder of Educational Coaching and Business Communications, a company that specializes in informational manuals for educators, parents, coaches and athletes.

The Staff

Outstanding high school and college coaches as well as players round out the coaching staff. Staff members are selected based upon their basketball knowledge and their ability to relate to the campers. East Coast Basketball Camps consistently assembles one of the finest camp staffs anywhere.

Tuition

Tuition at the East Coast Basketball Camp is $150.00 per one week session and includes a camp shirt. **Family discount of $10.00** for each additional child (immediate family) enrolled. To ensure that each child receives the individual attention necessary for improvement we often must stop accepting applications once we reach our capacity. To reserve your spot, please include complete payment with your application. Space is reserved on a first come basis.

(850) 264-3514
www.eastcoastbasketballcamps.com

Flyers

Flyers are an excellent marketing tool. It is a good idea to laminate your flyer if it will be outside. We post flyers anywhere we can including the following locations:

- Local schools

- Youth league fields & gymnasiums

- Post offices

- Camp facility

- Grocery stores

- Recreational facilities

- YMCA's

- Restaurants

- Video Stores

- Sporting Good Stores

- Little League Fields

Just as we do for our brochure we design our own flyer using a Publisher Program. (See next page). They are a great way to get the word out about your camp.

East Coast
Basketball Camps

July 10-14
West Stokes High School

**For Boys
& Girls
Ages 8-18**

Directed by Dan Spainhour

For more information call (850) 264-3323

E-mail—coachspainhour@eastcoastbasketballcamps.com

VISA   MasterCard   DISCOVER   AMERICAN EXPRESS

Register Online at
www.eastcoastbasketballcamps.com

Endorsements

Marketers rely heavily on testimonials. Camp directors should consider this as well. Be sure to use any endorsement you can. NCAA regulations prevent college coaches from endorsing a camp and from using their pictures on the brochure however, they can endorse a coach and his coaching ability. This is especially important when you are establishing your camp.

Try writing to any coach or player you may have a relationship with and requesting a short statement about your coaching and teaching abilities. A short note similar to the one below has worked for us in the past. Endorsements, even those from high school coaches, add credibility to your camp. You can use them in press releases, on your website and flyers. Keep in mind that you cannot put a college coach or player's picture or comments on your camp brochure and they cannot endorse your camp.

Dear Coach:

I am writing to request a favor—something I'm sure you get bombarded with everyday. I have started a basketball camp that I direct throughout the Carolinas as well as Florida and Virginia.

I was hoping that I could use you to "endorse" my coaching/teaching ability. A short sentence from you would be a tremendous help as we try to start our camp in areas where my name is not recognized. I certainly would understand if you prefer not to and I do not want to be bothersome to you but I know how much a short statement from you would mean to the initial development of our camps.

Thanks for your help. If I can ever do anything for you or your program, please do not hesitate to call.

Web Site

A web page is an excellent way for people to learn about your camp. Some service providers offer free hosting services or you can pay to have someone design a site for you. ECBC's service provider is Microsoft's bCentral. We designed the site ourselves using Microsoft FrontPage. Our site has been a tremendous asset to increasing our enrollment. It allows us to accept online registrations and payments via PayPal. You can see our complete site by visiting www.eastcoastbasketballcamps.com.

Newspapers

Many newspapers have sports calendar section that list area camps and clinics for no charge. Below is a letter we use to request a listing. Also, many papers have a special section published each spring that list the summer camps held in the area. Check with the paper in February or early March.

Dear Sports Editor,

I am writing to request a listing in your calendar section. I am the director of East Coast Basketball Camps. I would greatly appreciate it if you could run an announcement about our camp any chance you get between now & June 21st? Thank you!

East Coast Basketball Camp at West Stokes High School
Directed by Dan Spainhour
For: Boys & Girls ages 8-18; 8:30-3:00 each day
Tuition—$150
E-mail: coachspainhour@eastcoastbasketballcamps.com
For more information visit our Web site:
www.eastcoastbasketballcamps.com
or Contact: Dan Spainhour, Camp Director (phone)

The camp features quality fundamental instruction and specializes in individual attention in all phases of the game of basketball. All participants will learn the skills that will build the foundation for success in basketball. Campers are organized by age group and will participate in daily skills contests and league games. The camp closes on Friday with a league tournament. Every camper will receive a free camp T-shirt and an individual workout program that they can use on their own after the week has concluded.

I've also enclosed a news release about our camps. Please contact me if you have any questions or if I can provide additional information. Thank you so much for your help!

Sincerely,

Dan Spainhour
East Coast Basketball Camps
address
phone

Here is a sample of one of our listings in a newspaper's special camp section published in April of each year. Never underestimate the effects of free advertising!

East Coast Basketball Camps

Address: P.O. Box 11031, Winston Salem, NC 27116
Contact: Dan Spainhour
Phone: 239-254-1570
Email: coachspainhour@eastcoastbasketballcamps.com
Web Address: www.eastcoastbasketballcamps.com
Length of Day: 8:30am - 3pm
Extended Care: No
Session Dates: June 14-18, 2004 at West Stokes High School;
June 21-25, 2004 at Hartley Drive Family YMCA (High Point);
July 12-16, 2004 at YWCA of Winston-Salem
Ages Served: 8 - 18
Weekly Fees: $125 for West Stokes; For YMCA & YWCA camps
$125 members & $145 non-members

The camp features quality fundamental instruction and specializes in individual attention in all phases of the game of basketball. All participants will learn basketball skills that will help build the foundation for success in basketball. Campers are organized by age group and will participate in daily skills contests and league games. Every camper will receive a free camp T-shirt and an individual workout program.

News Releases (press release)

Creating a news release is a great way to get extra exposure. A news release or press release is a written correspondence sent to members of the news media for the purpose of announcing something claimed as having news value. Typically, it is mailed or faxed to editors at newspapers, magazines, radio stations, television stations, and/or television networks. They are a great way to use your endorsements that you have gotten about your coaching ability.

You can increase your chances of having your release taken seriously by following the format that most media outlets prefer for releases.

Format of a News Release:

Letterhead

Press releases should always be printed on a camp letterhead. You can design your own letterhead on your computer. The camp's name, web address, location address and phone number should be printed clearly at the top of the page.

Introduction

The words "FOR IMMEDIATE RELEASE" should appear in all caps in the upper left-hand margin of the page.

Title

Use an active headline to grab the editor's attention making them want to read on. Keep it short and descriptive. It should be centered, in all caps, and in bold.

Date and Location

This should provide the city you issue your press release from, and the date you're sending your release out.

Lead paragraph

The first paragraph should answer the who, what, where, when, and why, about the camp.

Other paragraphs

Other paragraphs should provide information about the camp. Add quotes that give a credibility and a personal touch to the release. Include your endorsements in these paragraphs. Conclude with a summary of the release.

End with news release standards

Skip two lines at the end of your release and center the symbols "###" or a "-30-" to indicate the end of the release. Journalistic standards have set basic parameters to define the end of a press release using one of these symbols. It should be centered directly underneath the last line of the release which indicates the end of a press release.

Preferably, a release should be one page—never more than 2 pages. See our standard release on the next page. Target every media outlet you know of within a 50 mile radius of the location of the camp. Any publicity is certainly worth the effort.

Oftentimes a newspaper, particularly a smaller one, will publish your entire release exactly as you sent it. Be sure to proofread your release before mailing.

East Coast Basketball Camps

7921 Umberto Court
Naples, Florida 34114

**East Coast
Basketball Camps**

*A Season In Words: A
Coach's Guide to
Motivation from the
Preseason to the
Postseason*

*How To Get Your
Child An Athletic
Scholarship: The
Parent's Ultimate
Guide to Recruiting*

*How to Run a
Basketball Camp: A
Guide to Directing a
Successful Basketball
Camp*

April 15, 2006

Contact Dan Spainhour
PO Box 11501
Naples, FL 34108
(239) 254-1570
Email:coachspainhour@eastcoastbasketballcamps.com

For Immediate Release

East Coast Basketball Camps Returns To Local High School

King, NC: East Coast Basketball Camps, a popular camp within the Carolinas, is once again coming to the triad. The following sessions are scheduled:
- June 14-18 at West Stokes High School, King, NC
  Tuition—$125
- June 21-25 at Hartley Drive Family YMCA, High Point, NC (Formerly HP Central YMCA)
  Tuition—$125 for members/ $145 for nonmembers
- July 12-16 at YWCA of Winston-Salem
  Tuition—$125 for members/ $145 for nonmembers

Each camp is for boys and girls ages 8-18 and will operate from 8:30-3:00 each day.

The camp is directed by Dan Spainhour. Coach Spainhour has been directing camps for over 18 years. He has received many awards during his illustrious coaching career, including three state championships and fourteen coach of the year honors. As a high school coach he won nearly 70% of his games. He has also coached at Florida State University and the University of Miami.

He is highly respected in the coaching profession and is the author of How To Get Your Child An Athletic Scholarship, a leading instructional guide on recruiting. He has instructed along side several top coaches including Duke's Mike Krzyzewski. "Dan is not only extremely knowledgeable about the game of basketball but he also has an amazing way of communicating with youngsters. It is a great combination," said Krzyzewski. "It is a privilege to endorse Dan Spainhour's coaching and teaching ability. He has been a tremendous coach at my camps."

The camp features quality fundamental instruction and specializes in individual attention in all phases of the game of basketball. All participants will learn the skills that will build the foundation for success in basketball. Campers are organized by age group and will participate in daily skills contests and league games. The camp closes on Friday with a league tournament. Every camper will receive a free camp T-shirt and an individual workout program that campers can use on their own after the week has concluded. " We are excited about bringing our camps back to the triad, said Spainhour. "The goal of our camp is to provide every camper, within a fun-filled atmosphere, the basic skills necessary to play basketball. We emphasize the fundamentals. Every camper will be shown what to practice and more importantly how to practice. Each camper will receive loads of individual attention. We want each and every camper to be a better player when the week is over."

To register for the camp or for more information call (239) 254-1570 or log onto
www.eastcoastbasketballcamps.com.
###

Local Publications

Almost every town has local publications such as monthly *parenting magazines, around town publications,* etc. Go to businesses in the area and look for magazine racks of local publications. Editors of these magazines are constantly on the lookout for material. Don't overlook these publications when you send your news releases. The more places you have your camp listed the better.

Always carry brochures and flyers with you. You never know when you'll come upon a place that would be a great location to put information about your camp.

Section Three

Before Camp

Registering Campers

Pre-registered campers are critical to the planning of your camp. Hiring coaches, placing t-shirt orders and other planning decisions are based upon projected enrollment. Because of the importance of having an idea of your enrollment, you may want to consider offering a reduced tuition to campers that register before the start of camp. I have found that no matter how long your camp has been in existence the majority of the registrations will come in right before the start of the camp so always plan for more than you expect.

As campers being to register for your camp, make sure you stay organized. ECBC sends a confirmation for every registration—see below. We prefer to do it via e-mail since it saves postage. For registrations that do not provide an e-mail we mail confirmation letter via regular mail.

E-mail Confirmation Note

Your application for the East Coast Basketball Camp has been received and accepted. You have been registered for the week of _____ at _____. The camp will run from 8:30 am to 3:00 pm Monday-Friday. You will receive more information prior to the camp. Thank you for your registration in our camp. I am looking forward to working with you this summer.

Sincerely,

Dan Spainhour
East Coast Basketball Camps
(239) 254-3333
www.eastcoastbasketballcamps.com

☝

Always request a read receipt to verify that they have received your e-mail.

Registration Organization

Organizing campers as their registration materials arrive allows you to stay on top of things. Take time to record registrations as they arrive. Early organization will make things go much smoother later as you prepare for the opening of camp.

Using a database allows you to easily sort campers which makes planning much easier.

First	Last	Street	City State Zip	Grade	Age	M/F	T-shirt	Session	Pd	Date	e-mail	Conf. sent
Kyle	Arganbright	1009 William Brown Lane	Kernersville, NC 27284	10	16	m	l	1	$125.00	3/19		3/19
Jacob	Hartle	1724 old Griffin Rd.	Rural Hall, NC 27045	3	8	m	yl	1	$125.00	3/19	ticky@aol.com	3/19
Bowen	Ammons	1137 King Rd.	Westfield, NC 27053	9	14	m	m	1	$120.00	3/21	tr0@hotmail.com	3/22
Zach	Hartle	425 Prince Albert Drive	King, NC 27021	6	11	m	s	1	$125.00	3/22	haom@alltel.net	3/22

Registration Letter

Send a registration letter two weeks before the start of camp. The purpose of this letter is to remind campers of the camp and to give them specific information about the camp.

Dear _____,

Your application for the _____ session of the East Coast Basketball Camp at _____ has been received and processed. I am looking forward to working with you and together we should have a great week of basketball and fun. We are excited about the week ahead and are working to make this session of camp an exceptional learning experience for you. The camp promises to be a fun experience.

With the opening of camp only a short time away, I would like to inform you of a few things:

- Check-in for camp will be from 8:00-8:30 on Monday morning.

- Camp will begin at 8:30 each morning and will end at 3:00 each day.

- Each camper should bring a bag lunch each day. Drinks will be available for purchase ($1.00) at the campsite. Lunches along with any valuables will be securely stored at the beginning of each day.

- Remember to come dressed to play basketball each day. Please wear only basketball shoes.

Please remember to bring with you the following when you arrive for check-in on Monday:

_____ Full Tuition Payment

_____ Partial Tuition Payment of _____

_____ Physical Form

_____ All of your camp information is in and processed. Thank you!

Again, we are really looking forward to working with you and helping to make you a better basketball player. See you at camp!

Coach Spainhour

First Day's Check-In

Proper planning for check-in on the first day of camp can help set the tone for the camp. Parents and campers show up on the first morning not knowing what to expect. The first impression of how the camp will be conducted occurs when the campers arrive. When parents see a well organized check-in with lots of supervision it can form a lasting impression about the camp. Here are some tips to make the check-in go smoothly:

- Have your counselor's arrive at least 30 minutes before check-in is scheduled to begin.

- Assign at least 2 people to check in campers. Try to get the most personable counselors you have.

- Depending upon the size of your camp have separate check-in tables—1 for campers whose last names begin with an A-L and another for last names starting with M-Z.

- Use the database spreadsheet you have prepared to easily locate campers and determine what materials they need to provide as they check-in.

- Have copies of the daily schedule available to give parents.

- As campers check-in counselors should be available to show them where to put their lunches, store their valuables and point them in the direction to go to wait until camp begins.

- It is important to be there as camp director to meet the parents and campers as they arrive and to answer any questions they may have. Parents want to see the director present when they arrive on the first day.

Walk-up Registration
(Campers who have not pre-registered)

As difficult as it may be to turn campers away, be very cautious about accepting a large amount of walk-up campers. It is easy to get caught up in the excitement of accepting campers only later to realize that you don't have enough personnel to provide proper instruction or supervision. If you plan for 40 campers and suddenly you have 65, while that can be good for the pocketbook it may hurt the quality of your camp. Decide your maximum number and plan accordingly. Once you reach that total, avoid the temptation to accept more campers.

Base your maximum number of campers on the following factors:

1. Number of counselors you have—try to keep the ratio to one coach for every 10-12 campers.

2. Available space—you don't want a small gym to be overcrowded.

3. Available T-shirts & other handouts.

4. Available equipment—basketballs etc.

Because of the time it takes to pay for the camp and complete the paperwork it is best to have a separate table at check-in just for walk-ups. Print out the forms on the following page and have them available for unregistered campers.

Each check-in table should have a safe place to keep payments that come in. It is easy for checks to be misplaced during the confusion that accompanies opening day registration.

Walk-up Registration Form

Name_____

Address_____

City, State, Zip_____

Location(s)_____

E-mail_____T-shirt size_____

Phone_____Emergency no._____

Age as of 1st day of camp_____Height____Grade entering_____

M/F____ School attending now_____

I waive and release _____Camp from any and all liability from injury and illness going to camp from home or while at camp or while returning home. I, as parent/guardian, have actual knowledge and appreciation of the particulars of the program and hereby voluntarily consent to said minor's participation, and assume the risk arising therefrom. I hereby give my permission for emergency medical treatment in the event I can not be reached.

I also understand that a physical examination within the 12 month period of the date the camper is scheduled to attend camp is required. By signing below I acknowledge that my child meets this requirement and does not have any medical condition that would prevent said minor from full participation in camp activities.

Signature of Parent/Guardian_____

Date:_____

Physicals

To ensure all campers meet the physical requirements, East Coast Camps requires a physical examination within the 12 month period of the date the camper is scheduled to attend camp. The parents/guardians acknowledge this with their signature on the camp application. A medical examination form is found in *Section 5—Camp Materials* that you can use.

Waiver Information from Parents

As previously mentioned, in today's litigious society you can never be too safe. ECBC requires all parents/guardians to sign a waiver. It is found on the camp application.

I waive and release East Coast Basketball Camps from any and all liability from injury and illness going to camp from home or while at camp or while returning home. I, as parent/guardian, have actual knowledge and appreciation of the particulars of the program and hereby voluntarily consent to said minor's participation, and assume the risk arising therefrom. I hereby give my permission for emergency medical treatment in the event I can not be reached.

I also understand that East Coast Camps requires a physical examination within the 12 month period of the date the camper is scheduled to attend camp. By signing below I acknowledge that my child meets this requirement and does not have any medical condition that would prevent said minor from full participation.

Signature of Parent/Guardian:_____

Date:_____

Lunches

One thing you will need to decide before camp is how you plan to handle lunch. Our format is for the campers to bring their own lunch. When the campers arrive each morning they place their lunch and any valuables they may have in a room that is supervised by a counselor. Once camp begins the room is locked and opened again at lunch time. At most of our camps we use the facilities' drink machines. At facilities that do not have machines we sell them from a concession stand that we operate.

Concessions/Merchandise

You may want to operate a concessions stand. We operate a camp bank which allows campers to deposit money into the bank and make purchases form their deposit. This eliminates the campers from having to keep up with the money during the day. We purchase our concessions supplies from Sam's Club before camp. We also sell various East Coast Basketball Camp merchandise such as t-shirts and shorts. It is a way to add to the financial bottom-line of the camp.

Early Arrivals/Late Departures

As you prepare for camp you will need to determine how you will handle campers that arrive early or the ones that leave late. Many parents have work demands that force them to drop their child off early or prevents them from picking up their child until late in the evening. I always arrive at least 1 hour and half before the start of camp and I stay until the last camper is picked up. You will need to develop a policy that is included in your brochure if you are not able to do this. Many camps charge a early drop-off and a late pick-up fee. For us, we have never had a problem because we plan to arrive early and stay late during camp .

Counselors' Meeting

It is a good idea to have a meeting with your counselors before camp begins. Sunday night before camp begins on Monday is an excellent time for the meeting. Trying to check-in campers, meet with the staff, assign duties etc. is nearly impossible if you wait until the first morning of the camp. Remember you never get a second chance to make a first impression and parents and campers form first impressions on how smoothly things are running on the first morning.

A typical agenda of the counselors' meeting should be:

- Welcome—goal of camp

- Distribute and discuss counselors' manual—*Each counselor is given a booklet—similar to the one starting on the following page— that has the daily schedules and responsibilities in it—see following page*

- Assignment of responsibilities—*complete Camp Personnel form found in Section 5—Camp Materials*

- Monday's check-in procedure

- Importance of enthusiasm.

- Thank everyone

East Coast Basketball Camps

Counselor's Manual

Counselor's Manual

(Come Dressed Like Basketball Coaches)

Dear Staff Member,

I want to thank you for your participation in East Coast Basketball Camps. By serving as a member of our camp coaching staff, you are providing young players the opportunity to learn and improve. The philosophy of our camp is to provide every camper within a fun-filled atmosphere the skills necessary to become a better basketball player.

Let's strive to make this the best basketball camp any of these participants will ever attend.

I look forward to spending this week of camp with you. Thank you in advance for your efforts to make East Coast Basketball Camps one of the finest camps in the country.

Instructors: Instructors will conduct the daily stations from 9:00-10:45. Instructors will record the names of the campers at their first station on Monday and then check attendance at their first station each day. Following the last station, the instructors will conduct the skills contest, which will take place with their first station at 10:45 each day.

Keep in mind the stations are more important than the games. Let the campers see that you are really concerned with them mastering the skills involved in your station.

Duties of the Instructors:

- Be at camp each day by 8:30

- Review your station's instructions before camp and ask me any questions you may have about what you are teaching.

- Be enthusiastic! Try to be as enthusiastic with your last station of the day as you are with your first.

- Sell the importance of what you are teaching.

- Avoid long lines. Keep everyone involved as much as possible. Remember that people learn by doing. Avoid talking too much.

- Check the attendance at your first station. I will be around each morning to see if there are any absences.

- After the last station of the day your first station will rotate back to you. At that time you are to conduct the skills contests and report the winner

(Continued on page 53)

(Continued from page 52)

to me as soon as you come to the camp meeting at 11:00.

- Allow the campers to have fun; but do not allow them to misbehave.

- Be positive in your approach to the campers.

- Report any injuries to me immediately.

- Meet at the end of camp each day to discuss the next day's plans.

Coaches: The success of our camp is directly related to the quality of our coaches. The young athletes look up to their coach. Try to learn as many names as soon as possible and establish a good relationship with the campers. The coach is responsible for coaching his team during the game.

Duties of the Coaches:

- Have a team meeting before your games and immediately afterwards.

- Be enthusiastic and positive at all times.

- Get the games started on time.

- Keep score of the games.

- NEVER use profanity.

- Referee your end of the court if we do not have referees assigned to your court.

- Ensure that your players are where they are supposed to be.

- Stress fundamentals and things taught during stations—not wins and losses.

- Report any injuries to me right away.

- Report any absences to me immediately.

- Inform all team members of game and film times.

- Give equal playing time. Do not establish a starting lineup—see numbering system on following page.

(Continued on page 55)

Game Substitution Schedule

Number the players on your team & use the following schedule to ensure equal playing time.

Players Sitting out

Rotation #	9 players	8 players	7 players	6 players
1	6-7-8-9	1-7-5	1-7	4
2	2-3-4-5	2-8-6	2-6	5
3	7-8-9-1	3-1-7	3-5	6
4	3-4-5-6	4-2-8	1-4	3
5	8-9-1-2	5-3-1	2-7	1
6	4-5-6-7	6-4-2	3-6	2
7	1-2-3-4	Repeat # 1	Repeat # 1	Repeat # 1
8	Repeat # 1			

Referee: The referee will officiate the games to the best of their abilities. They have the final say in any conflict that arises.

Referee Duties:

- Be at the games at least 5 minutes before they are scheduled to start.

- Keep the time for the final two minutes. Count aloud the final 20 seconds.

- Be serious about your job.

- Work hard—don't walk the floor.

- Call to the best of your abilities. Don't worry about mistakes or missed calls. Be decisive with your whistle and your calls.

- Report any camper behavior problems to the coach or me.

- NEVER say anything improper or out of line to a camper.

(Note: Some of our camps will not have referees. Coaches will officiate their end of the court for camps when officials are not employed.)

Runners: Runners are responsible for doing any odd jobs that may occur during the day.

Runner Duties:

- Make sure the lunch area is locked after camp begins and unlocked when it is time for lunch.

- Clean eating areas after lunch.

- Patrol the building to make sure campers are where they are suppose to be.

- Open the concession stand during lunch and after camp.

- Periodically check in with me to see if there is anything needed to be done.

Station Roster

Station_____   **Coach**_____

1. _____

2. _____

3. _____

4. _____

5. _____

6. _____

7. _____

8. _____

9. _____

10._____

Team Roster

Team_____   Coach_____

1. _____

2. _____

3. _____

4. _____

5. _____

6. _____

7. _____

8. _____

9. _____

10._____

Station 1 Ball Handling

Monday—Teach Techniques

    Ballhandling Drills:

        Control Dribble

        2 ball dribble

        finger tip tapping

        Yo-Yo dribble—up & back—Side to side

        figure 8—no dribble; figure 8 with a dribble

        around waist, head & legs—Ball quick

        Scissors

        Hike Drill

Tuesday—Same add—Clap—quick hands drills

        --Back toward passer

        --Passing off wall

        --Vertical Circle

Wednesday—2 line passing

    --Man in middle drill

   --Post feeding

  --Wall passing (practicing by yourself)

Thursday—Continue Drills

   --Dribble Tag

Friday—Review all Drills
   --Keep away

Station 2 Individual Offense

Monday—Triple Threat Position/Catching the basketball

--Jab step

--Jab & go

--Jab & crossover

--Jab & shoot

Tuesday—Crossovers—Use chairs or other obstacles

--Hesitation Move

--Fake crossover

--In & Out move

--Between legs/behind back/pullback crossovers

Wednesday—Inside moves:

--Drop Steps

--Up & under

--Shot Fakes

--Power Lay-ups

Thursday—Pullups & shot fakes

Friday—Speed Dribbles

--1 on 1 making a move to score

Station 3—Shooting

Monday

- Layups:

    1. Stress importance of developing both hands.

    2. Emphasize proper footwork.

    Use as few dribbles as possible.

- Transition Lay-ups:
    Start near half court and use only one dribble
    Have next person in line pass ball out in front & do lay up with no dribbles

- Power Lay-ups:
    Jump stop & power it in. Square shoulders to backboard. After doing it add shot fakes

- Getting fouled. Use off hand for foul hand

- Reverse Lay-ups (Mikan Drill)

Tuesday

- Form Shooting:

    1. Form lines close to the basket and work on technique—shoulders square, forearm perpendicular to floor, upper arm slightly above parallel to floor, ball off palm. Be a two eyed shooter.

    2. BEEF—balance, eyes on target, elbow in, follow through

    3. Emphasize it is not important to make or miss today. We are building their shot from the ground up.

    One hand then add guide hand.

(Continued on page 61)

(Continued from page 60)

Station 3—Shooting Continued

Wednesday

- Jump Shots:

    1. Same as yesterday but add the step in with the shooting foot. Teach one-two step in to shot.

    2. Raise the shot up as high as their age & size will let them. Teach elevation on shot.

- Motion Shooting:

    Teach shooting off v-cuts & screens. Have hands ready before the ball comes. One-two step into shot. Square-up outside shoe to prevent fading or rotating.

Thursday
- Free Throws:

    1. Emphasize a routine

    2. Positive visualization

    All good free throw shooters are slow & relaxed

Friday
- Shooting Games:
- Divide into two teams—first to ten wins
- Knockout
- 20 second shooting games

Station 4 Individual Defense

Monday—Defensive Stances

- Slides
- Machine Guns
- Wall Sits

Tuesday—Guarding the ball

- Mirror the ball
- Call Ball
- Call dead
- Containing the ball. Play shoulder to shoulder in the middle of the floor.

Wednesday—Guarding the ball continued

- Zig Zag
- Driving Lines

Thursday—Wing denial

- Teach ball u man
- Teach seeing both
- Teach passing lane
- Teach opening up on a back cut
- Teach wing denial into driving lines

Friday—Post defense & review

- Teach above the foul line—high side
- Below the foul line—low side

Station 5—Team Offense

Monday—Cutting

- Teach v-cuts

- L-cuts

- Back Cuts (basket)

Tuesday—Screening

- Jump stop into screen

- Call name & wait for screen

- 4 cuts—pop, fade, curl (the best one), basket

Wednesday—Motion Principles

- Pass & cut

  1. go away

  2. Screen

  3. basket cut

  4. Replace yourself

- Show a balanced floor—Teach ball reversals

- 5 on 0 motion

Thursday—Continue Motion Play

- 5 on 0

- 2 on 2 with an open coach

- 3on 3 etc. Keep teaching

Friday—Keep teaching how to play offense

Station 6—Inside Play/Rebounding

Monday—Teach posting up—Sit on opponent's thigh; show hand target

- Post feeding passing

- Chinning the ball

- Jump stops, Catch & chin

- Weakside flash; two foot jump stop (balanced & knees bent)

Tuesday—Drop steps—point lead foot and step to basket

- Flash, chin ball & do drop steps (baseline & middle)

Wednesday—Inside moves

- Up & under moves

- Show ball & go move

- Sikma move

- Jump hook

Thursday—Rebounding

- Teach blockouts & pivots.

- Hands high & lead with forearm.

- Chin the ball with elbows out

- 1 on 1 blockout into 3 on 3

- Teach being a good offensive rebounder—Don't accept being blocked out.

Friday—Live 1 on 1 Play in the Post

- Emphasize utilization of the moves learned during the week.

The opening of camp can be worrisome if you are not organized. More planning equals less headaches. A preparation checklist found in Section 5—Camp Materials will help guarantee that you have your bases covered and will help alleviate the anxiety of the opening of camp.

Section Four

Camp Format

Daily Schedule

After years of tweaking, East Coast Basketball Camps operates on a daily schedule similar to the following:

(Each activity is explained in detail in this section)

8:30   Morning Coaching

9:00   Stretching

9:15   Stations (Individual Instruction)

10:45   Skills Contest

11:00   Camp Meeting/Skills Contest Finals

11:15   Fundamental Session—How to Practice by Yourself

11:30   3 on 3 league play

12:00   Lunch

12:30   Set the Record Contests

12:50   Beat the Counselors Challenge

1:00 Afternoon Clinic/Guest Speaker

1:20   Shooting Seminar

1:30   Shooting Leagues/Hot Shot Contest

1:50   League Games

2:50   Camp Meeting & Dismissal

Morning Coaching—8:30-8:45

Opening with a brief lecture is a great way to convey your goals for each day. It is during this time I give the campers a quote for the day. I try to relate it to something that is relevant to that particular day. Counselors are instructed to periodically ask the campers if they know the quote of the day. At the close of each day, I ask the campers who knows the quote of the day. Some campers really get into it. Morning coaching is also the time when any instructions especially for that day are given. It's a great way to get the day started off on the right foot.

Below are examples of morning coaching segments:

Monday (Opening Lecture)

- Welcome

- Importance of eye contact

- Goals of our camp—what we want you to get out of it

- Our expectations of you

  - Be on time

  - Be enthusiastic

  - Be a good listener

  - Try

  - Have fun

- Daily schedule/ Explanation of contests

- Introduction of Staff

- Explanation of T-shirt & giveaways procedure

- Explanation of workout program & fundamental handouts that you'll receive

- Location of Restrooms

- Put trash away

- Concession Stand—Keeping food out of gyms

(Continued on page 71)

(Continued from page 70)

- If you have any problems see me or any coach—we're here to help.

- Quote of the day

Monday's quote(s)—*The biggest mistake a person can make is to be afraid of making a mistake.*

—*Nothing great was ever accomplished without enthusiasm*

Tuesday Morning Coaching

- Review of yesterday

- Quote of the day: *Those who have invested the most are the last to quit*

- Speech comparing practicing to investing into a bank account.

    —You get what you invest—you can only withdraw what you put into it,

    —Work now to get rewards later etc.

Wednesday Morning Coaching

- Review of yesterday

- Quote of the day: *The true measure of who we are is what we do with what we have.*

- Speech about avoiding excuse making.

    —You don't have to be the best just the best you can be

    —Excuses are for what didn't happen. Be prepared etc.

Thursday Morning Coaching

- Review of yesterday

- Friday's schedule—(tournament & dismissals)

- Quote of the day: *Knowledge is piling up facts. Improvement lies in their simplification.*

(Continued on page 72)

(Continued from page 71)

- Speech about how to practice properly

—Camps don't improve—they give knowledge. Knowledge becomes simple by practicing.

—Show how to practice by yourself. Tossing the ball etc.

Friday Morning Coaching

- Review of the week

- Today's schedule

- Quote of the day: *The time will come when winter will ask what you were doing all summer.*

- Speech on the importance of making good choices.

    —The choices you make—make you. When you don't practice you're making a choice not to get better etc. Be careful who you hang out with.

Stretching—9:00-9:15

I normally have our younger coaches lead stretching. Besides executing basic stretches needed to prepare for the day we also use this time for some fun activities such as the playing "coach sez". Played like "simon says" the coach calls out different fundamentals and the campers execute them. We do all sort of activities designed to get build enthusiasm leading in to the stations.

Teaching Stations—9:15-10:45 (6 stations-15 minutes each)

To place the campers into their station groups on the first day I have the campers line up along a wall from the youngest to the oldest. They are then divided into three divisions—normally 8-11, 12-15 & 16-18. Preferably, the stations are not coed, but in some instance the numbers require they be. If possible, each station should have no more than 10 campers in a group. There are six stations and each one lasts approximately 15 minutes. We try to have at least 2 stations from each division. A coach is assigned to each station. This coach is responsible for that first station each morning. He should record all members names and check attendance each day. He will also conduct skills contest with his first station. A whistle signals the end of each station and the campers then rotate to another coach to begin the second station. This allows the coaches to work with different campers.

Station Rotation

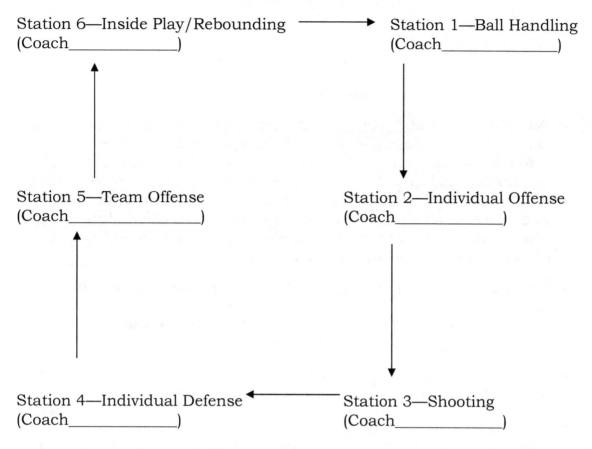

Station 6—Inside Play/Rebounding
(Coach_____)

Station 1—Ball Handling
(Coach_____)

Station 5—Team Offense
(Coach_____)

Station 2—Individual Offense
(Coach_____)

Station 4—Individual Defense
(Coach_____)

Station 3—Shooting
(Coach_____)

Skills Contests—10:45-11:00

After completing the final station the campers return to their first station group. Skills contests are then conducted with their first station. One winner is determined from each station group.

The Contests

- Monday's contest: <u>Knockout</u>—Campers line up at the free throw line with the first two campers in line holding a basketball. The first camper shoots and then the second camper. If they miss they must get the ball and quickly score before the person behind them makes a basket. If the person behind them makes it before they do then they are out. When they make it before the person behind them does they pass to the next person in line and go to the back of the line. Play continues until only one camper remains.

- Tuesday's contest: <u>Free Throws</u>—Each camper gets one practice free throw and then you begin. If the camper misses and the camper behind him makes it then he is out. Make it and he goes to the back of the line. Keep shooting until one is left.

- Wednesday's contest: <u>Three point shooting</u>—Shoot for 1 minute. The coach should rebound. Whoever makes the most wins.

- Thursday's contest: <u>1 on 1</u>—The campers line up. First camper at each basket will begin with a check of the ball to the next player in line. Play by the following guidelines:

  1. 3 dribble limit for older campers and 5 dribble limit for younger campers

  2. 5-second count and 3-second count are in effect.

  3. If a player is fouled in the act of shooting the basket counts,

  4. If a player is fouled on the floor check the ball at top of key to the next player in line. Defensive player rotates to back of line.

  5. The station's coach officiates at the basket.

  6. If the offensive player scores he keeps possession of the ball and checks the ball to the next camper in line. The defensive player rotates to the back of the line.

  7. If the defensive player stops the offensive player from scoring then he becomes the offensive player & checks the ball to the next camper in line. The offensive player rotates to the back of the line.

8. Play continues for allotted time. The camper with the most points at the end of the time is declared the winner.

9. Campers keep their own scores.

- Friday's contest:<u>30 Second shootout</u>—Each camper must make a shot from the following spots: (Use markers to designate the spots other than the lay-ups)

    1. Right side lay-up (Older campers must use right hand)

    2. Left side lay-up (Older campers must use left hand)

    3. Left wing

    4. Middle of lane

    5. Right wing

The camper must make a shot from each spot before they can advance to the next spot. If the campers makes a shot from all five spots they can then shoot from anywhere (including lay-ups). Each basket counts 1 point. Each camper has 30 seconds.

Camp Meeting—Skill Contest Finals—11:00-11:15

After the daily contest the campers come together for the skills contest finals. The finals held in front of the camp is something the campers enjoy and really get into. The station winners from each division compete against each other to determine a champion. The winner receives a certificate recognizing them as division champion and the winner of each station receives a certificate as well.

Fundamental practice Session—11:15-11:30

During this time period campers are shown different methods to practice fundamentals on their own. The purpose of this session is to show campers the proper way to improve. I instruct this with a counselor serving as a demonstrator. Below are our typical sessions.

Monday: *How to practice passing by yourself.*

- Show passing off a wall.
- Practicing hitting a target on the wall.
- Back to the wall—with back to wall, toss ball over shoulder and turn and catch. Works on quick hands.

Tuesday: *How to work on your shooting form.*

- Start close in—One hand.
- Gradually work your way out—two steps at a time.
- Add jump shot.
- Concentrate on form.

Wednesday: *How to practice game shooting by yourself.*

- Toss the ball out & catch & shoot.
- Toss ball high in air & make cuts & catch & shoot.
- Use a chair as a screener & toss, catch & shoot.

Thursday: *How to practice defense by yourself.*

- Mark off 15 feet & do slides.
- Cone in middle of a square & slide to cone & back alternating routine.
- Jump rope and quick feet drills.

Friday: *How to practice individual moves on your own.*

- Use a trash can or other object. Place it on court and execute moves.
- Add a second obstacle & make multiple moves.
- Show routine executing moves learned in stations.

3 on 3 league play—11:30-12:00

The 3 on 3 league takes place Tuesday-Friday. On Monday this time is used for 5 on 5 evaluation games so the coaches can inspect the talent in hopes of making the afternoon league teams as balanced as possible. For the evaluation games, the campers are divided into divisions according to ages. Preferably there are enough campers for 4 teams of eight players in each division. For the evaluation games the campers simply play 5 minute segments of 5 on 5 play and the coaches try to determine who the better players are. During lunch the coaches of each league get together and try to make a balanced league by placing the campers that received the highest evaluations on separate teams. The remaining of the campers in each age group are randomly placed on a team. These teams will be their 5 on 5 team for the week.

After Monday, this time will be used for 3 on 3 play. We believe that by allowing campers an opportunity to be on a 3-on-3 team as well as a 5-on-5 team we increase their chances for improvement. Unfortunately, in 5 on 5 situations some campers rarely touch the ball. In 3 on 3 play the campers are more involved. Try to limit the teams to four players. Each game is played for a certain time based upon the number of teams. It is best not to play to a predetermined score as some games make take too long. As we do in our league games, any foul in the act of shooting results in a made basket. If the basket goes in and a player is fouled then it is a three-point play (unless it's behind the 3 point line then it is worth four points). The last minute of the game is signaled by the camp administrator. At this time, the coach who is refereeing the court begins to keep the time. During this time all fouls are shot. All non-shooting fouls are one and one and shooting fouls are treated the way they are in a normal game.

Lunch—12:00-12:30

Campers are sent to lunch according to age group. Counselors are assigned to take the campers to get their lunch and stay with them while they eat. Preferably, the camp site has a lunchroom or a picnic area. Otherwise, the campers eat in areas outside of the gym.

Closely supervise lunch time. Most accidents/injuries occur during the free time at lunch.

Set the Record Contests—12:30-12:50

Our "set the camp record" contest has been instrumental in the success of our camps. The campers have an opportunity to enter into the East Coast Basketball Camp Hall of Fame which is posted on our internet site. Check our web site www.eastcoastbasketballcamps.com for our hall of champions. The campers eat it up! The campers have the opportunity to try their hand at different skills. They can try as many times as they like. A coach is assigned to each skill and similar to games at a county fair, the campers stop by and try to set the record. You can have as many categories as you like just make sure you have enough counselors to cover the contests. ECBC has the following:

- Consecutive Jump shots—The campers shoot until they miss. They must be at least two steps outside the lane.

- Lane Slides—Campers do defensive slides back and forth across the lane. Each time they touch the line it counts as one. They get 30 seconds.

- Consecutive Free Throws—Shoot until you miss

- Three pointers—The camper picks their own rebounder. They shoot for one minute

- Chippy Drill—Two campers partner up. A ball is placed on the two blocks of the lane. One player picks up a ball & shoots a lay-up & quickly gets the other ball & shoots it. Meanwhile the partner is rebounding and putting the balls back on the blocks. After 30 seconds they switch. The goal is to make as many as possible in one minute.

Beat the Counselors Challenge—12:50-1:00

Another aspect of the camp that the campers really enjoy is our beat the counselors challenge. During this time campers are invited to challenge a counselor to one of the contests conducted during the week. If a camper beats a coach the coach must do some pushups or run a sprint.

Afternoon Clinic/Guest Speakers—1:00-1:20

This time is for a guest speaker or an instructional video. One of the best ways to increase your camp's enrollment is to have quality people speak at your camp. If you can get a high profile player or coach to lecture at your camp you will immediately gain credibility. It can also be a catch-22 situation in that having a recognizable speaker can greatly increase your expenses. This can be difficult if you do not have a large enrollment. On the other hand, one of the best way to go from a small enrollment to a large one is by having a player or coach speak at your camp. Current NCAA rules prohibit paying college players more that you pay your regular coaches. If you have a college player speak you must pay him the daily amount you pay the other coaches and you must be prepared to provide the NCAA with your payroll should they ask for it.

👍

As much as speakers can add to a camp, poor unknown speakers can also take away from it. After a few years of running camps I had become a stickler for consistency. Our schedule called for a speaker each day at 1:00 and that's what I expected to have. We had players and coaches from Duke University, Wake Forest and outstanding high school coaches speak to our campers. At one location, we were having a hard time finding speakers. Instead of finding something to replace that portion of camp I was determined to find speakers. I finally lined up some local speakers who had never worked or even attended a basketball camp before. Needless to say they were not very inspiring. By Wednesday I had campers coming to me asking if they had to have a speaker that day. At the close of camp as I was giving each camper a workout program and thanking them and their parents for choosing our camp a few parents called me to the side and told me how much they loved the camp because of our commitment to teaching the fundamentals but they asked if I ever considered skipping the speaker portion of the day. The point is—be flexible. If you can't line up quality speakers then don't have any. Campers do not want to sit through a long, uninspiring speech when they want to be playing basketball.

Shooting Seminar—1:20-1:30

Our shooting seminar is designed to built the proper jump shot from the ground up. Because of the importance of developing proper shooting form we add this afternoon session even though shooting skills are taught in the morning. The campers are placed at the baskets and their shots are evaluated.

Here are our shooting seminars:

- Monday—Brief Instructional Video of correct shooting forms/Campers then practice BEEF (Balance, Eyes on Target, Elbows in, Follow Through) as a group without a basketball.

- Tuesday-- Building a shot

    One hand against the wall
    Sitting down in pairs & shoot to each other w/ 1 hand
    Lying on the floor w/ 1 hand
    One hand shots in close

- Wednesday--Form Shooting using the legs

    Flip Shooting (practicing shooting from the catch)
    Jump shots—Stepping into shot. Shoot at top of jump

- Thursday-- Free Throws—teach routine

    Motion Shooting—Show how to practice shooting using v-cuts/screen etc.

- Friday—No seminar

Shooting Leagues/Hot Shot—1:30-1:50

After the evaluation games on Monday morning the campers are placed onto a team. This will be their 5 on 5 team for the shooting leagues and for league games. For the shooting leagues there will be 4 quarters with each quarter lasting one minute. Each team will shoot from 4 spots—1 each quarter. Change spots each day. Keep up with points. The team that is ahead at end of game is the winning team for that day. Keep records for the week.

For hot shot there are 5 spots. You also get to shoot 2 shots inside the lane. Campers are not required to shoot from each spot but they get 5 bonus points if they make one from each spot The play starts at the foul-line & continues for one minute. Keep score all week. A blank scorecard is found in the

(Continued on page 81)

(Continued from page 80)

appendix for you to use. The campers with the highest scores at the end of the week are the winners. They also have a chance to enter the Hall of Champions if their score breaks the camp record.

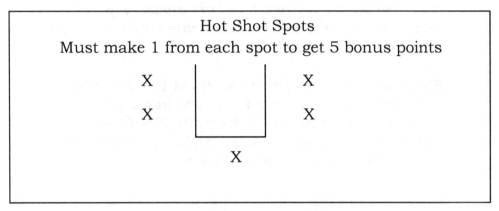

League Games—1:50-2:50

We schedule so each team plays two games a day. Your schedule will depend upon the number of courts you have and the size of your camp.

Game Rules

The games last approximately 20 minutes running time. We do not keep a visible clock—see next page. Approximately five minutes before the game is scheduled to end the camp administrator signals to everyone that two minutes remain. At this time the referees begin keeping the time by counting down in their head and calling out the remaining time every ten seconds or so. The clock stops on all whistles in the final two minutes. In the final two minutes all fouls result in shooting fouls—either one & one on non-shooting fouls or two shots for fouls in the act of shooting. Non-shooting fouls before the final two minutes are taken out of bounds.

Before the final two minutes fouls in the act of shooting results in a made basket. Any foul in which the basket is made is a three point play unless it is a three point shot and then it is worth four points. Coaches keep score. Substitutions are made every five minutes and are signaled by the camp administrator. All teams must play man to man defense. Teams are not allowed to press full court until the final two minutes of the game.

☝

- *No matter how much planning or organizing you do you will find it is sometimes difficult to stay on schedule. One way to help is to NOT keep the time for the games on a visible clock. This will allow you to add or shorten game times without anyone feeling short changed.*

- *Since the clock stops in the final two minutes be sure to allow enough time so the game ends on schedule. To accomplish this the final two minutes should be signaled at least five minutes before you want the game to end.*

Video Session

When teams are not playing they go to a film room and watch a highlight tape. This is something that is enjoyable such as the highlights from the previous year's Final Four. See examples below. On Thursday the campers see a video of a game—NBA or college. At this time, the coaches point out various fundamentals taught during the week and show whether they are being executed correctly or incorrectly by the players on the screen.

Video Sessions:

Monday—Final Four Highlight Tape

Tuesday—NBA Finals Highlights

Wednesday—Florida State Highlight Tape

Thursday—Game video—Coaches instruct. Campers watch a real NBA or college game and the coaches point out fundamentals and skills taught during the week. It helps for campers to see the skills being executed in real game situations.

Camp Meeting & Dismissal—2:50-3:00

After the final game of the day the campers come together for the final meeting of the day. The following is discussed:

- The quote of the day

- Examples of what you learned

- Quick review of the day's teaching

- Handout of certificates to the day's contest winners

Closing Camp on the Last Day

The last day's schedule is a little different from the other days. Camp ends with an afternoon tournament. Invite parents to attend. The closing of camp is a special time and parents like to be a part of it.

- Final Camp Meeting: Immediately before the start of the tournament the campers are brought together and are explained the tournament and checkout procedure. This is the time to give final instructions and stress what you've been trying to teach during the week. It is best to hold the meeting before the tournament because after the tournament it is hard to hold the campers attention.

- Check out procedure: Following the teams last game of the tournament the teams are brought to a designated area where the camp administrator thanks each camper personally and gives them their t-shirts, workout program and fundamental checklist.

Tips for painless day to day operations

- *If possible have a trainer available. When one is not available have someone, preferably you, who is knowledgeable about first aid. Have a fully equipped first aid kit.*

- *Hire enough help to allow you the freedom to handle problems and/or injuries as they arise.*

- *Train someone to handle Monday's registration. Many parents will want to discuss things with you the first day. If you are busy registering campers it can easily frustrate parents who may be in a hurry to get to work. Be available to meet and greet the parents as they arrive.*

In the following sections you will find materials and forms for your camp. The format is basically the same for all of our camps but they are adjusted slightly from location to location to allow for differences in enrollment and facility size. Also, remember to adjust things according to your goals and objectives.

Section Five

Camp Materials

Camp Personnel

Week: _____ Date:_____   Site:_____

Director's Assistant:_____

Monday's Registration: _____

Instructors:

    Station 1—Ball Handling_____

    Station 2—Individual Offense_____

    Station 3—Shooting_____

    Station 4—Individual Defense_____

    Station 5—Team Offense_____

    Station 6—Inside Play/Rebounding_____

Coaches:

    League:Girls (WNBA)

        Team 1_____

        Team 2_____

        Team 3_____

        Team 4_____

    League: 8-12 year old boys & girls (ACC)

        Team 1_____

        Team 2_____

        Team 3_____

        Team 4_____

(Continued on page 88)

(Continued from page 87)

League: 13-18 year old boys (Big East)

        Team 1_____

        Team 2_____

        Team 3_____

        Team 4_____

Referees: (minimum of 6)_____   _____

                        _____   _____

                        _____   _____

Morning Stretching_____

Videotape (optional)_____

Set the Camp Record drills

        3 pointers_____

        Lane slides_____

        Chippy Drill_____

        Consecutive Jump shots_____

        Consecutive Free Throws_____

Runners_____

Concessions_____

Guest Speakers:

        Monday:_____

        Tuesday:_____

        Wednesday:_____

        Thursday:_____

Camp to do list

Session_____Location_____ Date_____

Site confirmation_____

Concessions_____

Basketballs_____

Other camp equipment_____

Counselors Confirmed_____

Counselor's Meeting Scheduled_____

Prepare counselor meeting (counselor's manual/agenda)_____

Mail registration letter_____

T-shirts_____

Insurance_____

Prizes/Giveaways_____

Daily Schedules_____

Teaching Stations Planned _____

Speakers_____

Game schedule_____

Videos_____

My lectures_____

Fundamental Practice Sessions_____

Workout handouts_____

Fundamental Handouts_____

Game videotaping sessions_____

Site preparation_____

Skills Contests_____

First Day's Schedule

8:30	Welcome/Morning Coaching/Expectations
9:00	Stretching
9:15	Place campers in stations
9:25	Stations Trail Run—Make sure the campers have the rotation
9:30	Stations
10:45	Skills Contests
11:00	Camp Meeting/Skills Contest Finals
11:15	Fundamental Practice Session—How to Practice by Yourself
11:30	5 on 5 evaluation games
12:00	Lunch—Coaches select teams
12:30	Set the Record Contests
12:50	Beat the Counselors Challenge
1:00	Afternoon Clinic/Guest Speaker
1:20	Shooting Seminar
1:30	Shooting Leagues/Hot Shot
1:50	League Games
2:50	Close/Recognition of Daily Winners

Daily Schedule

8:30	Morning Coaching
9:00	Strectching
9:15	Stations
10:45	Skills Contests
11:00	Camp Meeting/Skills Contest Finals
11:15	Fundamental Practice Session—How to Practice by Yourself
11:30	3 on 3 league play
12:00	Lunch
12:30	Set the Record Contests
12:50	Beat the Counselors Challenge
1:00	Afternoon Clinic/Guest Speaker
1:20	Shooting Seminar
1:30	Shooting Leagues/Hot Shot
1:50	League Games
2:50	Close/Recognition of Daily Winners

Health Exam Record for Campers

Name:_____   Birthdate:_____

Phone:_____   Parent: _____

Address:_____

Emergency Contact:_____ Phone: _____

To Be Completed By The Specified Medical Practitioner:

Date of Exam: _____ Signature of Examiner:_____

_____May participate in all basketball camp activities

_____May participate except for:

_____

Medical Information pertinent to routine care and emergencies:

_____

Is the individual taking prescription medications? YES NO If yes, indicate prescriptions:_____

Does the individual have allergies? YES NO
Explain:_____

Is the individual on a special diet? YES NO
Explain:_____

This camper/staff is up-to-date on all the following routine childhood immunizations currently recommended by the American Academy of Pediatrics and National Advisory Committee on Immunization Practices:

	Yes	No
Measles		
Mumps		
Rubella		
Chickenpox		
Tetanus		
Hepatitis B		
Diphtheria		
Pertussis		
Polio		

Print name of medical care provider: _____
Medical Care Provider's address: _____
Medical Care Provider's: City/Town _____ ST ____ Zip _____

Basketball Camp

This certificate is presented to

In Recognition of:

Camp Director

Date

Game Scheduling

Scheduling obviously depends upon the number of campers and the number of courts that you have available. In our efforts to have each camper play two games a day we try to limit our leagues to four teams and we always try to have a minimum of four courts. Of course this is not always possible and we sometimes adjust our daily schedule and start our games earlier in the afternoon. Below are round robin schedules for 6, 5, 4, and 3 teams in a league. On the following page is a grid to assist in completing your week's schedule.

6 Teams Round Robin Schedule

Round One	Round Two	Round Three	Round Four	Round Five
1-2	1-4	1-6	1-5	1-3
3-4	2-6	4-5	6-3	5-2
5-6	3-5	2-3	4-2	6-4

5 Teams Round Robin Schedule

Round One	Round Two	Round Three	Round Four	Round Five
1-Bye	1-4	1-6	1-5	1-3
3-4	Bye-6	4-5	6-3	5-Bye
5-6	3-5	Bye-3	4-Bye	6-4

4 Teams Round Robin Schedule
3 Teams Round Robin Schedule

Round One	Round Two	Round Three
1-2	1-4	1-3
3-4	2-3	4-2

Round One	Round Two	Round Three
1-Bye	1-4	1-3
3-4	Bye-3	4-Bye

Game Schedule Grid—3 Leagues, 4 courts

LA=League A, LB=League B, LC=League C
T1=Team 1, T2=Team 2, T3=Team 3, T4=Team 4
Example:LA/T1 vs. LA/T3 = League A Team 1 vs. League A Team 2

Day	Time	Court One	Court Two	Court Three	Court Four	Film
Monday	1:50	LA/T1 vs. LA/T3	LA/T2 vs. LA/T4	LB/T1 vs. LB/T3	LC/T2 vs. LC/T3	Teams not Playing
	2:10	LC/T2 vs. LC/T1	LC/T4 vs. LC/T3	LB/T4 vs. LB/T2	LA/T3 vs. LA/T2	Teams not Playing
	2:30	LB/T1 vs. LB/T2	LB/T3 vs. LB/T4	LC/T1 vs. LC/T4	LA/T1 vs. LA/T4	
Tuesday	1:50	LC/T2 vs. LC/T4	LC/T3 vs. LC/T1	LA/T1 vs. LA/T2	LB/T4 vs. LB/T2	Teams not Playing
	2:10	LB/T1 vs. LB/T4	LB/T2 vs. LB/T3	LA/T4 vs. LA/T3	LC/T4 vs. LC/T3	Teams not playing
	2:30	LA/T1 vs. LA/T3	LA/T2 vs. LA/T4	LB/T1 vs. LB/T3	LC/T2 vs. LC/T1	
Wednesday	1:50	LC/T2 vs. LC/T3	LC/T1 vs. LC/T4	LA/T1 vs. LA/T4	LB/T2 vs. LB/T3	Teams not playing
	2:10	LB/T1 vs. LB/T2	LB/T3 vs. LB/T4	LA/T3 vs. LA/T2	LC/T3 vs. LC/T1	Teams not playing
	2:30	LA/T1 vs. LA/T2	LA/T4 vs. LA/T3	LC/T2 vs. LC/T4	LB/T1 vs. LB/T4	
Thursday	1:50	LA/T1 vs. LA/T3	LA/T2 vs. LA/T4	LB/T4 vs. LB/T2	LC/T1 vs. LC/T4	Teams not playing
	2:10	LC/T2 vs. LC/T1	LC/T4 vs. LC/T3	LB/T1 vs. LB/T3	LA/T1 vs. LA/T4	Teams not playing
	2:30	LB/T1 vs. LB/T2	LB/T3 vs. LB/T4	LC/T2 vs. LC/T3	LA/T3 vs. LA/T2	

Camp Game Schedule—4 teams in each division/4 courts

Leagues—ACC (Duke, State, Wake, UNC)—8-12 year old boys & girls;
Big East—(Syracuse, UConn, Pitt, St. Johns) 13-18 year old boys; WNBA—(Mystics, Comets, Sparks, Sting)13-18 year old Girls

Monday Evaluation Games at 11:30—ACC—Court One; Big East—Court Two, WNBA—Court 3.

Day	Time	Court 1	Court 2	Court 3	Court 4	Film
Monday	1:50	Mystics / Comets	Sparks / Sting	Duke / State	UConn / St. Johns	Teams not Playing
	2:10	UConn / Syracuse	Pitt / St. Johns	Wake / UNC	Comets / Sparks	Teams not Playing
	2:30	Duke / UNC	State / Wake	Syracuse / Pitt	Mystics / Sting	
Tuesday	1:50	UConn / Pitt	St. Johns/ Syracuse	Mystics / Sparks	Wake / UNC	Teams not Playing
	2:10	Duke / Wake	UNC / State	Sting / Comets	Pitt / St. Johns	Teams not playing
	2:30	Mystics/ Comets	Sparks / Sting	Duke / State	UConn / Syracuse	
Wednesday	1:50	UConn/ St. Johns	Syracuse / Pitt	Mystics / Sting	UNC / State	Teams not playing
	2:10	Duke / UNC	State / Wake	Comets / Sparks	St. Johns / Syracuse	Teams not playing
	2:30	Mystics / Sparks	Sting / Comets	UConn / Pitt	Duke / Wake	
Thursday	1:50	Mystics / Comets	Sparks / Sting	Wake / UNC	Syracuse / Pitt	Teams not playing
	2:10	UConn / Syracuse	Pitt / St. Johns	Duke / State	Mystics / Sting	Teams not playing
	2:30	Duke / UNC	State / Wake	UConn / St. Johns	Comets / Sparks	

Friday Tournament

	Court One	Court Two	Court Three
1:00	Big East 1 vs. 4	Big East 2 vs. 3	WNBA 1 vs. 4
1:30	ACC 1 vs. 4	ACC 2 vs. 3	WNBA 2 vs. 3
2:00	Big East consolation	ACC consolation	Big East Championship
2:30	WNBA championship	WNBA consolation	ACC championship

Camp ends Friday following your last tournament game. Checkout will be done with your team at which time you will receive your camp shirt and workout program.

Hot Shot Competition Scorecard

There are 5 spots & if a player makes one shot from each spot they get 5 bonus points. You get to shoot 2 lay-ups. Play starts at the top of the key. Time will vary depending upon time available. We will keep score all week.

Name_____

Monday's Score_____   Tuesday's Score_____

Wednesday's Score_____   Thursday's Score_____

Friday's Score_____   Total_____

Name_____

Monday's Score_____   Tuesday's Score_____

Wednesday's Score_____   Thursday's Score_____

Friday's Score_____   Total_____

Name_____

Monday's Score_____   Tuesday's Score_____

Wednesday's Score_____   Thursday's Score_____

Friday's Score_____   Total_____

Name_____

Monday's Score_____   Tuesday's Score_____

Wednesday's Score_____   Thursday's Score_____

Friday's Score_____   Total_____

Name_____

Monday's Score_____   Tuesday's Score_____

Wednesday's Score_____   Thursday's Score_____

Friday's Score_____   Total_____

Ball handling Fundamentals & Teaching Outline

Ball handling Teaching Points:

- Dribble with head up

- Keep dribble at waist level or below

- Control ball with finger tips and not the palm

- Stay low

- Keep dribble protected with non-dribbling hand

- Push the ball from one hand to the other quickly and low for crossover dribbles.

- "Low-to-high-next dribble by". When executing a move take the dribble very low then put the next dribble after the move by the defender.

Basic fundamentals:

- Balance
- Head up
- Feet shoulder width apart
- Stay low
- Fingers control the ball
- Let the wrist do the majority of the work
- Keep the dribble below the waist & keep it firm

Drills:

- Control Dribble—Stay low, use one arm for protection, dribble with fingertips.
- Two ball dribble—Dribble at same time & alternate.
- Finger tip tapping—Tap ball back & forth between fingertips.
- Yo-Yo dribble—dribble ball up & back & side-to-side, like it's a Yo-Yo.
- Figure 8 dribble—dribble between legs.
- Figure 8 between legs (no dribble)—take ball as quickly as you can between your legs.

(Continued on page 100)

(Continued from page 99)

- Loops—Take ball around your head, back, chest & legs as fast as you can. Be ball quick.
- Scissors—Dribble ball between legs while walking.
- Hike drill—hike ball between legs from front of the body to back with out dropping the ball.
- M-dribble—Sitting down with legs spread apart, dribble the ball between legs.
- One knee figure eight—Dribble between legs & around the body while on one knee/ alternate knees.
- High/low—with 2 balls dribble one ball above the waist while dribbling the other one below the knee. Alternate.
- Cradle—Hold ball between the legs with one hand in front of the leg and the other behind. Change the position of the hands without letting the ball hit the ground.

Passing Fundamentals and Teaching Outline

Chest Pass

- Two hands on the basketball.

- Hold ball in the chest area, with hands placed firmly on the sides of the ball and elbows out.

- Step toward your target and deliver the ball to your teammate above his waist and below his shoulders.

- Extend your arms and let the ball come off your finger tips.

- Follow through with fingers pointing at your target and thumbs down.

Bounce Pass

- The bounce pass is made the same way as the chest pass except you aim at a spot on the floor so that the ball will bounce up to the receiver's waist.

- Aim for a spot approximately midway between you and the receiver.

- Use the pass to get the ball by a defender's hands in a scoring area.

Overhead Pass

- The ball is held at head level with two hands firmly on the side.

- Step toward your target, release the ball and follow through with fingers pointing toward the target and thumbs down.

- The overhead pass may be used to outlet the ball after a rebound, pass against pressure, or get the ball to the low post.

Hook Pass

- The hook pass is a one handed pass used to defeat pressure or pass to the post when defended.

- Keep two hands on the ball as long as possible for control.

- To make a right-handed hook pass, step around the defense with the left foot and pass the ball.

Basic Offensive Moves Fundamentals and Teaching Outline

Triple Threat—The ready stance for basketball.

- The three options are: dribble, pass & shoot.

- Stand with your feet slightly staggered and the weight on your balls of your feet.

- Knees are flexed and the upper body is leaning forward ever so slightly.

- The player's shooting arm should be in an L shape and his shooting wrist and hand should be in a shooting position.

- Play the game low.

Jab step

A jab step is a short, quick move to create space between an offensive player and his defender.

- From the triple threat position the player should take a short, quick step directly at the defender.

- As the player steps at the defender he should move the ball to a protected position beside his body.

- A player should jab with the foot that is slightly staggered forward.

- Players should be able to execute the following moves from the jab step:

   1. Jab & Go—the most common move. The player jabs quickly & then goes past the defender using the body to close out the defender. Use this move when the defense is playing you very closely. Player should be able to go right and left

   2. Jab & Shoot—if the defender reacts to the jab step by retreating then a player should be able to shoot right away. The jab step must be short enough that a player remains on balance and is able to perform a jump shot without having to regain his/her balance.

(Continued on page 103)

(Continued from page 102)

3. Jab & crossover—if the jab step causes the defender to move in the direction of the steps the player should counter it with a quick crossover step. Use the lead leg to closeout the defender and always dribble the ball with the outside hand—the hand that is away from the defender)

Jump-stop

- Anytime a player first receives a pass or when he stops from a dribble he should jump-stop into the triple threat position.

- When the player's feet touch the ground they should be parallel to each other.

- The weight should be equally balanced between both feet.

Pivot

- To establish a pivot foot a player should first use a proper jump-stop.

- If done correctly a jump-stop allows a player to choose either foot as his pivot foot.

- Use the pivot to improve angles for passing, dribble or shooting.

Fakes

There are two basic fakes and both serve the same purpose—try to get the defender out of position so you can quickly gain an advantage.

- **Pass Fake** (ball fakes)—Players should become comfortable using pass fakes. The important point is to make the fake seem real.

- **Shot fakes**—A good shot fake is a critical ingredient in the repertoire of good offensive players. Quickly move the ball upwards as if you are going to shoot. Also move your head and eyes upward but don't come out of your triple threat position. Stress the importance of the players using shot fakes and staying low so they can quickly drive past the defenders.

Shooting Fundamentals and Teaching Outline

Lay-up

- Start by positioning players one step away from the basket.

- Imagine there is a string attached to your shooting arm and your leg. When attempting a right hand lay-up the elbow rises as the right leg is lifted.

- The left hand is used to support the basketball.

- Elevate off of your left leg for right hand lay-ups and off your right leg for left handed lay-ups.

- Keep eyes on target.

- Encourage players to jump like a rocket on take off and not a jet plane. By jumping in more of an upward path the ball is less likely to be tossed too hard off the backboard.

Reverse Lay-up

- The technique for a reverse lay-up is similar to a regular lay-up.

- As the player's body moves to the other side of the basket encourage them to use soft hands and snap the wrist to flip the ball out of the shooting hand toward the basket.

- Avoid the habit of throwing the ball. Younger kids often do this because of a lack of strength.

Power Lay-up

- Used when a player is defended to the basket or when he is moving at a high rate of speed and he needs to gain control before shooting.

- The player should jump-stop properly.

- Elevate like a rocket and use the non-shooting hand to protect the ball from the defender.

- If the defender fouls the player the non-shooting hand should receive the contact.

- Shoulders should be square to the basket. Do not open them toward the defender.

- Add shot fakes to power lay-ups. For shot fakes close to the basket the ball should not move because it is too easy for defenders to slap the ball away inside. Inside fakes should be head and shoulder fakes with very little ball movement.

Jump-hook

- To properly attempt a jump-hook a player should be close to the basket. It is a good skill to master because it is a shot that is very difficult to block.

- Have players rotate their body so that the shoulder of the non-shooting arm is pointing directly at the basket.

- Move the non-shooting hand so that it ends up directly between the basket and the ball.

- The shooting hand continues to face the basket.

- The forearm should be vertical and the ball should be directly over your shooting shoulder.

- To become as tall as possible, your shooting arm should be fully extended, with only a slight bend at the elbow.

- To protect the ball, keep the non-shooting hand fully extended, until the ball is well on its way to the basket.

- When shooting a right hand jump-hook establish your left foot as the non-pivot foot. Then, take a step with it, jumping vertically and shooting as you complete the step.

Jump Shot

- The ball should sit on the finger pads of your shooting hand and not on the palm.

- The wrist should be flexed.

- The non-shooting or guide hand should be on the side of the ball for better ball control.

- The elbow is bent and should be directly under the ball. When waiting for the pass, be in a "ready position," knees bent, feet pointing at the basket, hands ready with fingers pointing up,

(Continued on page 106)

(Continued from page 105)

prepared to receive the ball.

- Eyes should be locked on your target.

- As you jump, reach up, and release the ball with a flick of the wrist and a good follow through. The follow through will give you good reverse rotation and make your shot soft on the rim.

- Teach BEEF (balance, eyes on target, elbow under ball and follow through).

Additional Drills and Contest Ideas

Figure 8 test: The camper takes the basketball and passes it through the legs and around the legs in a figure 8 shape. The ball does not hit the floor. Each time a figure 8 is completed they score a point. Number of figure 8's in a minute.

Figure 8 dribble test: Same as above except with a dribble

Dribble Speed Test: The camper dribbles across the width of the floor with their power hand and then they dribble back with their weak hand. Take 2 trips. Timed Test

Lay-up Test: The camper starts at the elbow. They dribble in and shoot a lay-up then they dribble back and repeat. One minute for each side. Add total made.

Spot shooting Test: 5 spots (both wings/both corners/foul line) Count number of shots it takes to make one from each spot.

Defensive Slides Test: Campers start at a corner of the baseline and slide center of baseline under the basket and slide to foul line and back and then to half-court and back and then back to corner. This is a timed test.

Mikan Drill (1 minute)—Camper starts under the basket & shoots a right hand reverse lay-up & then rebounds it and shoots a left hand reverse lay-up. Older players must use both hands.

+4; -4—Every shot you make counts 1 point—every missed shot counts –2. If you get to +4 points before –4 you win. Shots are taken outside the lane. Keep going until you have one winner

Around the world challenge. Campers shoot a long shot (3 pointer for older campers) and a shorter shot from 5 spots—Left baseline, Left wing, top of key, right wing, right baseline. They must make the shot before they advance to the next spot. Three misses from the same spot disqualifies the camper. The objective is to get around the world with the fewest number of shots possible.

32 point shooting—5 spots (top of key, both wings and both baselines). The camper shoots a 3 pointer (worth 3 points) 2 pointer (worth 2 points) ; & a lay-up (worth one point) from each spot. He then finishes with 2 free throws. The objective is to get the highest score. 32 is a perfect score. You may want to only shoot from a two spots (14 points) as this drill takes a lot of time.

Basketball Terminology

Back door - cut made to the basket against tight denial defense.

Back screen - a pick set from behind on a defender away from the ball.

Body to body - the way you should drive by defenders and come off a pick.

Box out or block out - move used to keep the offensive rebounder away from the backboard.

Close out - moving out to pick up a man with the ball.

Contest - raising hand to defend a jump shot.

Deny - to keep offensive player from receiving a pass.

Down screen - screen set in the low post area by a wing player.

Drop step - movement made with basketball when taking the ball to the basket on a post move.

Elbow - the area where the lane and the foul line meet.

Five man - center.

Four man - power forward.

Gap - space between two defenders.

Helpside - position of defenders two passes or more away.

High post - foul line area.

Influence -defensively force the ball to one side of the floor.

Low post - area within six feet of the basket.

One man -point guard.

Over play - defensive denial of a pass.

Paint - foul line area.

Penetrate and kick - offensive man drives into the lane and passes to an open teammate.

Perimeter - the area 15-20 feet from the basket.

Pick and roll - two man play where a screen is set for the dribbler.

Pivot - movement made while keeping one foot planted.

Pull through - crossing the ball from one side of your body to the other.

Short corner - area half way between the basket and the corner.

Strong side - the side of the floor the ball is on.

Tandem - one player lined up behind another.

Three man - small forward.

Trap - double team of the man with the ball.

Two man - shooting guard.

Weak side -the side of the floor away from the ball

Wing - area behind the three point line and the foul line extended

Zone defense - defense where each player is responsible for an area on the floor.

Marketing Letters

On the following pages are marketing letters we have sent to churches and local sponsors. Feel free to use them verbatim changing only your name, camp name and other appropriate details if you feel you can benefit from them.

Letter to Churches

Dear Youth Minister,

I want to inform you of an exciting opportunity that we are providing for youth in your area. Several years ago I founded East Coast Basketball Camps. The goal of the camp is to provide every camper, within a fun-filled atmosphere, the basic fundamentals necessary to play basketball. Our camp emphasizes skill development while at the same time stressing the importance of character development, dedication and the value of hard work. We firmly believe that the values imparted at our sessions make a difference in the lives of our campers.

I would like to invite your youth to attend our camps. I have enclosed some brochures as well as a flyer about our camps. You can find more information at www.eastcoastbasketballcamps.com.

I have dedicated my career to helping young people develop physically, mentally, and spiritually through athletics. I am as excited about the advancement of East Coast Basketball Camps and the benefits it provides for children as anything I have ever done. I hope you will consider informing your members about our camp so we can continue to have an impact on young people in your area. Thanks for your help!

Sincerely,

Dan Spainhour
Camp Director

Letter to Sponsors

Dear Prospective Sponsor,

I want to inform you of an exciting opportunity that we are providing for youth in your area. Several years ago I founded East Coast Basketball Camps. The goal is to provide every camper, within a fun-filled atmosphere, the basic fundamentals necessary to play basketball. Our camp emphasizes skill development while at the same time stressing the importance of character development, dedication and the value of hard work. We firmly believe that the values imparted at our sessions make a difference in the lives of our campers.

East Coast Basketball Camps seeks out sponsors from the community to help defray the costs of facility rentals, hiring first-rate instructors and additional operating expenses. Your sponsorship will   ensure that we can continue to provide each camper with quality instruction, a t-shirt, a fundamental instruction book, and a basketball reference manual at a cost that they can afford. In return, we provide you with:

- Maximum exposure—We run 11 sessions during the summer—one each week from June 2nd through August 8th and a special evaluation camp in the evenings from June 23-27. Last year we averaged nearly 100 campers consisting of boys and girls ages 8-18. Parents and other adults attend many of the camp sessions. League games as well as the final tournament provides a perfect setting to generate publicity for your company.
- Advertise in one of the most effective venues—youth sports. A recent report in *The Kiplinger Letter* identified youth sports as good places to attract attention.
- Logo on camp brochure.
- Logo on Sponsor banner that will be displayed at all camp sites.
- Logo and link on camp web site.
- One free camp scholarship for a week at any East Coast Basketball Camp.
- Logo on instructional booklet given to all campers.
- Logo on fundamental reference booklet given to all campers and parents.

We also offer a title sponsorship that will provide you naming rights and other attractive incentives. Please contact us if you think you may be interested in a title sponsorship.

I have dedicated my career to helping young people develop physically, mentally, and spiritually through athletics. I am as excited about the advancement of East Coast Basketball Camps and the benefits it provides for children as anything I have ever done. I hope you will consider supporting the camp so we can continue to have an impact on young people within the community.

Sincerely,

Dan Spainhour
Camp Director

Sponsorship Information

Championship Package-$300

- Logo on camp brochure

- Logo on Sponsor banner that will be displayed at all campsites

- Logo and link on camp web site

- One camp scholarship for a week at any East Coast Basketball Camp

- Logo on instructional booklet given to campers

- Logo on fundamental reference booklet given to campers and parents

- Advertise in one of the most effective venues—youth sports

Information

Sponsor Name_____

Street Address_____

Contact Person_____

Telephone_____Fax_____

E-Mail_____

Web Site_____

Please submit a logo.

Make checks payable to: East Coast Basketball Camps

Interested in Title Sponsorship? E-mail us at

coachspainhour@eastcoastbasketballcamps.com or call (239) 123-4567

The following sections are handouts that we give each camper when they checkout on the final day of camp. The first is a fundamental checklist that serves as a written review of what was taught during the week. You can use it to help with your instructional preparation.

The second handout is a workout. It gives the camper a program to follow to improve upon the skills learned during the week.

Feel free to copy verbatim and distribute as needed.

Camp Fundamental Checklist

Fundamentals of Basketball

Here are some of the basic fundamentals of the game of basketball. We believe that mastering these fundamentals is essential to your development as a basketball player. It is essential for players to have an understanding of the game and its fundamentals. We hope this will be of use to you.

Ball handling & Passing

Types of passes that should be mastered:
1. Chest
2. Bounce
3. Overhead
4. Baseball
5. Post Feeds

Fundamentals of Passing:
- Step into pass.
- Make firm, sharp passes (no rainbows).
- Call person's name to whom you are passing.
- Make a good follow though.
- Use ball fakes (fake high—throw low & vice versa)
- Post feeding specifics:
  Get down with the pass.
  Look into post for one full count.
  Throw away from defense—throw to target hand.

Fundamentals of Catching:
1. Always catch the ball with two hands.
2. Catch the ball with your eyes.
3. Get your feet under you when your receive the ball.
4. Get into triple threat position.
5. Give a hand target & call for the ball.
6. Look the ball into your hands.

Types of dribbles that should be mastered:
1. Equal use of hands. There should not be a noticeable dominate hand when dribbling the ball.
2. Spin dribble.
3. Crossover dribble.
4. Behind the back.
5. Speed dribble

Fundamentals of Dribbling:
1. Keep head up at all times.
2. Use the fingertips and not the palms
3. Use the body to protect the dribble.
4. Low hard dribble.
5. On behind the back dribble—pull the ball through and make sure you have changed direction
6. For speed dribbles—push the ball out front. Try to cover the most amount of space with the fewest dribbles possible.

Defense

Defensive Fundamentals:
A. Stance:
1. Stay low.
2. Be comfortable. Don't hunch your back. To get into a stance place your palms on your knees and lower your back keeping your arms straight. Remove your hands.
3. Stay balanced.
4. Slide without crossing feet.
5. Stay on balls of feet—don't get flat footed.
6. Practice wall sits to keep your back straight.
7. Have active hands.
8. Stay in your stance until player no longer can dribble. Then come out of your stance and get big.

B. Talk:
1. Call help when on helpside.
2. Call "dead" when dribble is picked up.
3. Talk through screens.

C. Seeing Both:
1. Always see both the ball and your man.
2. Point to the ball and to your man.

D. Ball-You-Man Position:
1. Stay between your man and the ball. See both ball and man.
2. When your man is one pass away be in the passing lane—the imaginary line between the ball and your man & closer to your man. This is called "on-the-line; up-the-line."
3. When your man is 2 passes away (not as close to the ball) you are further from your man.
4. The court is divided into 2 sides. Imagine a line running from one basket to the other. This line dissects the court into equal

halves. Ballside is the side the ball is on and helpside is the other side. When you are on ballside you are in the passing line. When you are on helpside you have one foot in the free throw lane so you can help when the ball drives toward the basket.

E. Guarding the ball:
1. Pressure the ball by mirroring the ball with your hands.
2. Stay in your stance until your opponent no longer can dribble.
3. Influence your man toward the sideline. Keep them out of the middle of the floor.

F. Guarding your man when he does not have the ball:
1. Always move as the ball moves.
2. Move into the direction of each pass.
3. Always see both ball and man.
4. If the ball is dribbled toward you—help by fake trapping & then recover to your man. This is called helping and recovering.

Offensive Fundamentals

A. Lay-ups—It is essential that everyone master lay-ups with both hands.
1. Right hand—jump off left foot.
2. Left hand—jump off right foot.
3. High jump, don't long jump.
4. Power lay-ups—jump stop with both feet & square shoulders with the backboard. Power the ball with both hands out in front of the body. Use the non-shooting hand to draw the foul. Use a power lay-up when there is a defender near.

B. Jab Steps—From triple threat position you should be able to execute a jab step.
   Fundamentals of a jab step:
1. Keep the jab short & quick.
2. Stay on balance.
3. Let the defense dictate your move—if they are close to you then jab & go by. If they are playing you loose then jab & shoot. If they move in the direction of the jab then jab and crossover.
4. Step through with your lead leg and close out the defense.
5. Throw yourself into the move.

C. V-Cuts

V-Cut Execution Phase

1. Cut to basket ___	6. Turn on ball of foot ___	12. Meet the pass ___
2. Concentrate on two-count move ___	7. Push off to outside ___	13. Catch ball with two hands ___
3. Use deception and timing ___	8. Shift weight ___	14. Use one-two stop ___
4. Three-quarter step with inside foot ___	9. Long step with outside foot ___	15. Land on inside foot first ___
5. Knee flexed ___	10. Outside hand up as target ___	16. Front turn to middle ___
	11. Continue cut outside ___	17. See the rim and defender ___

from "Basketball Steps to Success" by Hal Wissel

18. Triple-threat stance ___

Screening

A. Fundamentals of screening:
1. Call and signal for the person you are screening for.
2. Jump stop into your screen and set a solid pick.
3. Shape up after setting a screen. The person most likely to be open is the screener.
4. The person using the screen should set the defense up by doing a "mini' v-cut. Wait for the screen & cut off of it.
5. You should make 1 of 4 cuts when using a screen:
   - Curl cut—when you curl around the screen toward the basket.
   - Pop cut—when you pop toward the ball.
   - Fade cut—when you come to the screen and then fade away. Use this cut when the defense overplays the screen.
   - Back cut—go to the screen & then backdoor to the basket. Use this cut when the defense jumps above the screen.

Shooting

1. The ball should rest on the pads of your fingers and the fingers spread comfortably to provide the best control. There should be enough space between your palm and the ball that two fingers can fit in the space. Shoot with your fingers & not the palm.

2. Eyes on the target. Aim for the middle of the basket or just over the front of the rim.

3. Square your shoulders to the basket to maintain balance. Aligning your shoulders allow for proper direction with your shot.

4. Do not cock the ball. Keep the space between your wrist and your shoulder the same. If you bring your wrist too close it means your are throwing your shot instead of shooting it.

5. Keep the shooting elbow parallel to the floor. Lift the elbow to get lift on your shot.

6. The knees should bent and the feet shoulder width apart to maintain balance. Extend legs to get lift. Generate distance with your legs and not your arms.

7. Use your off-hand as a guide. Do not let it interfere with your shooting hand.

8. Lift the ball above the head to give yourself a shooting "window" in which you can see the target. Do not place the ball directly in front of your eyes.

9. Extend your wrist and execute a good follow through.

10. Remember Beef—Balance, Eyes, Elbow, Follow-Through

Shot Problem	Cause	Solution
Regularly misses to the left	• Elbow may be out of line to the outside of the body • Feet may be pointed to left of basket • Poor balance • Shoulders improperly aligned	• Focus on shooting line of elbow. • Align feet & shoulders. • Do "freeze" drills—get ready to shoot on the move & freeze before shooting to check alignments
Regularly misses to the right	• Elbow may be out of line to the inside of the body. • Feet may be pointed to right of basket • Poor balance • Shoulders improperly aligned	Same as above
Regularly misses to one side or the other—not consistent	• Poor balance • Guide hand interference	• Freeze drills for balance check • Shoot without guide hand. Start close to basket & work on form. Only add guide hand until you're comfortable with the one hand. • Add guide hand but on shot freeze it so it doesn't move. Focus on the action of the guide hand.
Misses are straight but are hitting the front or back of the rim.	• Check arch of shot. • Check distance between shooting wrist & shoulder. Don't cock the ball.	• Shoot with more arch than usual. Overexaggerate it. • Shoot with a firm wrist & then extend the follow through.
Misses even though everything appears to be executed properly.	• Check eyes. What are you looking at? • Check how the ball is held in hand • Eyes following the flight of the ball instead of being locked on the target.	• Focus on what you see are you shoot. Call out what part of the rim you're looking at. • Make sure ball is not resting on palms • Lock eyes on front part of rim.

Rebounding

Fundamentals of Blocking Out:
1. When a shot is taken immediately put your hands high.
2. Put your foreman in the chest of the person you are blocking out.
3. Pivot on your man—keep contact with him.
4. See the ball and anticipate where the ball will come off the rim.

Free Throw Shooting

Fundamentals of Free Throws:
1. Stay balanced at the line
2. Use a routine
3. Positive self-talk
4. Create the shooting line with the elbow under the ball
5. Sight the target
6. Bend slightly at the knees and shoot.
7. Use good arch
8. Follow through

These are some of the basic fundamentals of basketball. As you advance you will find more and more fundamentals that must be mastered. However, everyone needs to have a solid foundation upon which to build upon. Once you've mastered the fundamentals included here you will have a solid base which you can build your game on. Best of luck!

Basketball Camp

Workout Program

Dear Camper,

Thank you for attending our camp! It is my hope that our camp was a fun week and that it was a learning experience for you. I also hope that you have caught some of our enthusiasm for the game of basketball and you want to improve your skills. This workout will help you get results for your efforts.

This workout is designed to improve your overall game. The drills included here were shown to you during the week of camp. I encourage you to concentrate on all phases of your basketball game. Too often young players concentrate only on a few phases of basketball because they consider themselves forwards, centers or guards. I encourage you to start thinking of yourself as a basketball player and not as a certain position. That will come later. For now, work on all fundamentals of the game. Two primary goals of this camp was to show that basketball is fun and to show you exactly how to go about getting better. I hope we accomplished the first goal and if you follow this workout I know we will accomplish the second one!

> *"The image of a champion is someone who is bent over drenched in sweat to the point of exhaustion—when no one else is watching."*

> *"It is not the hours that you put in that counts...what counts is what you put into the hours."*

I wish you the best with your basketball career. Good luck, work hard and most of all have fun!

Camp Workout Program

The following is a workout program that will prove very beneficial if you follow it and work hard at it. If you follow the schedule faithfully, you will become a vastly improved player. Furthermore, the mental discipline that you must develop to follow this program will stay with you the rest of your life.

Summary

Without a doubt, the more you practice the fundamentals the better you will become. All you need to do is set a side time each day and run through the following drills. Mix up your practice session each day so you don't get bored with the same routine. The key is to do them, preferably every day. The drills are set up so you don't need a partner to workout.

The Program

Station I   Lay-ups/Passing/Ball handling

Lay-up drills:

1. Right hand

2. Left hand

3. Down the middle

Format:

- Go full speed from half court

- Make 5 lay-ups from each spot

- After you've made the lay up dribble back hard to the appropriate location & repeat

- Add reverse lay ups & power lay ups

- This is also a good conditioner

Checkpoints:

- Proper angle

- Head up

- Dribble with outside hand

- Where you take off from

- High jump off opposite foot

- Put the shot high on the board

Passing

Passes: Chest, Bounce, Overhead, Baseball, Feeding the post, Fake up, pass down, Fake down, pass up, Behind the back.

Drills:

Find a wall that can support your passes. Tape or mark a spot on the wall and work on all the passes trying to hit the spot. Use your imagination and see the spot as your teammate's hand.

Format:

- Spend 30 seconds on each pass

- Place emphasis your off-hand

Checkpoints

- Back spin

- Roll thumbs through the ball

- Step to the pass and step to meet the pass

Ball Handling

Drills

- Pound the ball

- Fingertip control drill

- Pass around the body

- Figure 8 dribble

- Dribble around legs

- Dribble with eyes closed

- Pass around legs

- Dribble sitting down

- Dribble lying down

- Dribble with 2 balls

Format

- Simply do each drill for 30 seconds.

Checkpoints

- Be quick but not in a hurry

- Start slow and gradually increase speed

- Don't look at the ball

- Stress fingertip control, improving your off hand and improving hand-eye coordination

STATION II REBOUNDING (5 MINUTES)

Drills

- 5 and in—toss ball off backboard 5 times & put it in

- Toss ball off backboard and tap it in with your right hand. Then use your left hand.

- Toss ball off back board & tap it with your right hand against the board as many times as you can. Repeat with your left hand. Younger players should tap it against a wall.

- Mikan drill (hook drill)

- Try to jump up and touch the backboard 10 times in a row as quickly as you can. Land on balance and jump without having to gather yourself.

Checkpoints

- Keep your hands high on all the drills

- Stay on balance

- Explode upward with each jump.

- Jump quickly. Quick jumpers are more effective than high jumpers.

STATION III INDIVIDUAL DEFENSE (10 MINUTES)

Drills

- Defensive slides up, down, and around the court

- Line jumps

- Machine gun drill

- Wall sits

- Jump rope

- Box drill

Format

- Do each drill two minutes each.

- Emphasize quickly moving from drill to drill

- These drills are killers if done properly

- You should shoot free throws after doing these drills while you're tired

Stance Checkpoints

- Feet shoulder width apart

- Drop your backside to get low

- Back should be relatively straight

- Head up

- Hands out

Slides Checkpoints

- Don't cross your feet

- Don't hop

- Step with foot closest to the directions you are moving

- Slide with the other foot

- Pivot to change direction

STATION IV SHOOTING

Drills

- Shoot with only one hand—work on form

- Shoot while lying on floor

- Shooting off the pass

- 20 second shooting—as many shots as you can get off in 20 seconds. Count down in your head.

- Shooting off the dribble—take 3 dribble make the last dribble hard & let it take you into your shot.

- Imaginary 1 on 1—make move & shoot jump shot

- Shooting off v-cut

- Shooting off screens

- Free throws

Format

- If you miss a shot always follow it up until you make it

- Each drill should consist of a minimum of 10 shots and at

least 3 different spots on the floor.

- Use your imaginations—act as if you are in a game

- For shooting off pass & v-cut: toss the ball high into the air make your cut & catch the ball off the bounce & shoot

- For shooting off screens—set up a chair or trash can etc. Imagine that it is your teammate screening for you. Toss the ball out & make one of your four cuts off the screen. (the 4 cuts are: pop, curl, fade, & back)

- Shoot free throws when you are tired

Checkpoints

- Balance—feet shoulder width apart and one slightly in front of the other.

- Shooting hand—fingertips spread and the ball does not touch the palm. Shooting arm—elbow in.

- Non-shooting hand does not affect the shot

- Release it while you have good vision

- The shot—pop your elbow for greater arc

- Keep eyes on target—don't follow the flight of the ball

- Good follow through

- Use your legs for power

Other points of emphasis

- Warm-up slowly from close in and gradually move out

- Always square your shoulder to basket

- Make last dribble an extra hard one

- Know your range

- Don't dip the ball after catching a pass

- BEEF—**B**alance, **E**yes on target, **E**lbow In, **F**ollow-through

STATION V MOVES ON THE MOVE

Part I—Dribble Moves

- Low driving dribble as if you are being guarded

- High speed dribble as if you are being guarded

- Crossover dribble

- Change of pace

- Spin dribble

- Fake spin dribble

- Behind the back

- Between the legs

Part II—Shooting moves on the move

- Dribble pull up

- Speed dribble pull up

- Shot fake one dribble relocation shooting

- Pull back dribble into shot

Drills

- Full court dribbling

- End up with a lay-up or a jump shot

- Add chair or another obstacle as a defender & dribble toward the obstacle & make move around it

Format

- Simply go up & down the court working on your moves. If you only have a half court then do them within the area that you have

- This is a great conditioning drill and it makes your workout game-like

- Head up

- Protect the ball

- Be quick but not in a hurry

- Remember and practice shooting checkpoints when you shoot after making your moves on the move

Station VI Stationary Moves
Moves after the catch & before you have started to dribble.

Moves

- Strong side drive

- Crossover drive

- Jab & shoot

- Strong side jump shot

- Crossover jump shot

Drills—Simply execute each move one after the other

Format

- Start in the lane & toss the ball out & catch it

- Turn & face the basket

- Execute your move

- Add obstacles such as a trash can, chair etc. Use your imagination—act as if you are being guarded

Checkpoints

- Always catch in triple threat position

- Always turn & face the basket using a pivot

- Short jab; followed by a long one

- Stay on balanced

- Close out the defender

- Knife toward the basket on a long step or a crossover move.

STATION VII INSIDE MOVES

Drills

- Drop steps

- Up & under moves

- Square up & do stationary moves

- Shot fakes

- Square up jump shots

Format

- Post up with your back toward the basket & toss the ball to you as if you are receiving a pass

- Use your imagination—act as if you are being guarded

Checkpoints

- Wide base

- Demand the ball

- Give hand target

- Sell your shot with a fake

- Stay on balance

EACH PRACTICE SESSION SHOULD END WITH FREE THROWS

It is my hope that this guidebook was helpful to you and that you have as much fun running your camps as I have had. I wish you much success with your camps and in all of your future endeavors. I hope you meet all of your objectives and exceed all of your expectations. All the best always!!

Dan Spainhour
coachspainhour@eastcoastbasketballcamps.com.

Want Additional Copies or Know Someone Who Can Benefit From This Guide or One of Our Other Products?

Visit www.ecbcommunications.com or Order Here

Make your check payable to ECBC and return to:

Educational Coaching & Business Communications
7921 Umberto Court
Naples, FL 34114

Name_____

Address_____

City/State/Zip_____

E-mail_____

Phone_____

Item	Quantity	Price
How To Run A Basketball Camp		$19.95
How To Get Your Child An Athletic Scholarship:The Parent's Ultimate Guide to Recruiting		$24.95
A Season In Words: A Coach's Guide to Motivation from the Preseason to the Postseason		$19.95
	Total Order	
	Florida Residents Add 6%	
	Total	

9 780615 143293